KEVIN KEEGAN

Portrait of a Superstar

KEVIN KEEGAN

Portrait of a Superstar

JOHN GIBSON

W.H. ALLEN · LONDON

Typeset by Sunrise Setting, Devon
Printed in Great Britain by
Mackays of Chatham Ltd, Kent
for the Publishers, W.H. Allen & Co. Ltd,
44 Hill Street, London W1X 8LB

ISBN 0 491 03363 X (W.H. Allen hardcover edition)
ISBN 0 86379 081 X (Comet books softcover edition)

Quotations from the following books are reproduced by kind permission of the publishers: *Against The Word* by Kevin Keegan, Sidgwick and Jackson; *Bob Paisley, An Autobiography*, Arthur Barker; *I Did It The Hard Way* by Tommy Smith, Arthur Barker.

Frontispiece: A dog's life. Kevin with a greyhound named after him and Newcastle United's sponsors — Blue Star Keegan.

CONTENTS

Acknowledgements

I WOULD LIKE TO THANK THE NEWCASTLE Chronicle and Journal Ltd, Thomson Regional Newspapers and their paper in Bangkok for their considerable help with the photographs. Also all the managers and players who kindly gave some of their time. And, most important of all, Kevin Keegan for giving football followers throughout the world so much pleasure over the years.

KEVIN KEEGAN

Portrait of a Superstar

CHAPTER ONE

We're in heaven, we've got Kevin

THE SCENE WAS FIT FOR THE ENTRANCE OF an American president. Reporters, hard bitten, perhaps cynical with a seen-it-all-before attitude, whispered excitedly amongst themselves in anticipation. Radio men fidgeted, making certain that their mikes were plugged in and their tape recorders capturing every word. And the ITV crew were scurrying everywhere with that special nervous energy which marks a live television broadcast.

The time was 6.30 p.m. on August 19, 1982. The place a private room in the plush Gosforth Park Hotel on the outskirts of the Newcastle city centre.

Newcastle United were about to make what they unashamedly have called 'the greatest signing in our history'. They had landed Kevin Keegan against all the odds.

11

To understand what Keegan's signing meant at that precise moment you need to understand what football means to a Geordie. It isn't a pastime or even a sport. It's a religion. And Newcastle United are right at the centre of that religion. A club with a past distinguished by a succession of achievements, St James's Park had regularly been packed to capacity with fans basking in the glories achieved by such folk heroes as Bill McCracken, Hughie Gallacher, Jackie Milburn, Bobby Mitchell, Frank Brennan, Len White and Malcolm Macdonald. But the famous Magpies had fallen on bad times. Relegated to Division Two, they were little more than a colourless middle-of-the-table side forced to live in the past.

Then amazingly, unbelievably, they signed the biggest box office draw in British football.

Even Russell Cushing, a respected secretary, forgot himself a little as he got to his feet and, borrowing some of Muhammad Ali's outrageous razzmatazz, announced: 'We're in heaven, we've got Kevin.' It may have been unlike a man used to the more sombre atmosphere of the St James's boardroom, but then wasn't everyone caught up just a little?

Keegan swept into the room, self assured, smiling as the bulbs flashed and the TV commentator's voice shot off at machine-gun rate. Ever the diplomat, King Kev was wearing a black and white tie with the initials 'NUFC' on it.

He talked easily, quickly, with the assurance of a man who knew he was in charge. A natural manipulator.

'Yes, he felt promotion was on . . . no, there was never any doubt once United had moved in for him . . . certainly he would be moving his family up to the North East . . .'

Keegan, knowing the pride Geordies feel for their own, sold himself magnificently to perhaps the hardest audience of all — the media men. And his *pièce de resistance* was a winner as surely as one of his whiplash shots or cunning headers. His dad was a Geordie!

Joe Keegan was born at Hetton-le-Hole in County Durham and had only found his way down to Doncaster when jobs in the mines became so scarce in the North East. That made Kevin a half Geordie coming home to his folks, did it not?

Behind the half-drawn curtains down the left hand side of the room young United fans pressed forward, their faces flattened and contorted against the panes of glass. The chant which was to ring round Tyneside for the next two seasons began: 'Kee-gan ... Kee-gan ... Kee-gan ... '

United manager Arthur Cox, outwardly calm and stony faced as usual, signalled to the commissionaire to draw back the curtains completely and the noise rose to a crescendo. Keegan waved and smiled his acknowledgement. Later a side door was to be opened and a policeman called to help supervise a queue of kids seeking Keegan's autograph.

As the formal proceedings broke up I nipped out to the gents. A Newcastle director followed me, looking elated but pale.

When I offered my congratulations he said: 'We've gambled. My God, we've gambled. This signing will either make us or break us at the bank.'

Keegan's contract had — in fairness to both player and club — been restricted to a single year. Keegan had to see for himself that he hadn't dropped a clanger and signed for a club with little real ambition and United, up to their eyeballs in hock, had to make sure they had got their sums right.

Though both parties were to pooh-pooh the idea of Keegan's wages topping £3,000 a week there was no question that with all the extras he had just made himself England's top wage-earner for a season.

United chairman Stan Seymour and manager Arthur Cox were the inspiration behind a signing which startled the soccer world and left the majority of clubs green with envy.

United had swooped almost a week before when the word on the grapevine was that a disillusioned Keegan might well be ready to leave Southampton for a fresh start.

On the Saturday, five days before KK signed, Cox and Newcastle's board of directors met secretly to discuss a dramatic bid to land England's captain. When Seymour initially told his fellow directors of the plan one actually laughed in his face. Keegan for Newcastle appeared that ridiculous even to those within St James's!

But already United had a trump card in their hand. About a year before, Cox, convinced that what a soccer-mad but depressed area like Tyneside needed was a top performer, had taken Keegan's agent Harry Swales to lunch. He had stressed to Swales that when Kevin's contract was up at Southampton and he was a free agent United would be interested. It was a shrewd move because Keegan remembered and was impressed by Newcastle's patience and perseverance.

Opposite page: The greatest signing in the club's history — Kevin Keegan joins Newcastle United, watched by manager Arthur Cox.

Battle plans laid, United were to deal themselves another trump card. They phoned their main sponsors, Newcastle Breweries, to ask for their full support. The idea was that the breweries would greatly top up Keegan's wages in an entirely separate deal by also signing him on to do promotional work. Keegan and a brewery was an unlikely liaison with Kevin a teetotaller and totally opposed to beer advertising. But it was to work like a charm.

So at eight o'clock on the Monday morning — August 16 — United's party left the Newcastle Central station bound for a secret meeting with Keegan in London. The party consisted of Stan Seymour, Arthur Cox, Russell Cushing, commercial manager David Hogg, Newcastle Breweries' sales director Alastair Wilson and their marketing manager Ron Woodman. Seymour, Cox and Cushing had opted out of Newcastle's pre-season trip to Madeira to press on with the transfer and Keegan flew in from Holland, where Southampton were touring, to meet his agent and Newcastle's contingent.

The £100,000 transfer fee had already been fixed — by Kevin. He'd had the figure written into his Southampton contract a couple of years before on joining them from Hamburg, a ploy he was to adopt again with Newcastle.

And Southampton boss Lawrie McMenemy, a Geordie himself, had greatly helped Seymour once he knew the parting of the ways was inevitable. Stan had sought guidance on Keegan's wages and the way to handle such a delicate transfer and Lawrie had obliged.

Alastair Wilson of the breweries recalls: 'We all had lunch with Kevin Keegan and Harry Swales in a London hotel and then Ron Woodman and I left the room so that Newcastle could talk to Keegan privately. Afterwards we had private talks with Kevin and United's party were

16

Stan Seymour, who masterminded the Keegan
signing with Cox.

kind enough to leave us alone.

'At that stage they were preliminary talks on how we
could use Kevin in the North East should he sign for
Newcastle. It was made plain then that Kevin would
never be pictured with a pint in his hand but that was
fine by us. We didn't want to use him in direct consumer
advertising because it was imperative to retain his clean-
cut image with the young people. Instead we wanted to
utilize his ability in public relations in going out and
meeting his fans.'

Keegan himself felt that here lay the new challenge
that he needed at thirty-one years of age.

'The minute I talked to Newcastle and shook hands I knew that was it,' he said. 'I only talked to two clubs — Manchester United and Newcastle United — but I could have talked to thirty. I knew Newcastle wanted me and I'd never felt so excited for a long time — since I first met Bill Shankly. You don't have to sell Newcastle to anyone, especially if you have played up there.'

Kevin had to return to Holland to play for Southampton against Utrecht. The Saints had been guaranteed £15,000 for the game but only if England's skipper was in their side.

Secrecy was still the order of the day though speculation was mounting. When the unsubstantiated news first appeared in the papers that Keegan might sign for either Manchester United or Second Division Newcastle it was treated with derision by fans on Tyneside. A publicity stunt to keep us all happy, it was said in the pubs and clubs.

Another Division Two club which had fallen on hard times, Charlton Athletic, decided to find out for itself what was really happening. They could see the value of a player of Keegan's stature at the gate and ambitious chairman Mark Hulyer and manager Ken Craggs flew to Holland to talk to McMenemy. They need not have bothered — Lawrie told them a secret deal with Newcastle had been completed. They were too late.

A bitterly disappointed Hulyer was to turn to another former European Player of the Year, the Dane, Allan Simonsen, to try and match Keegan at the gate but his gamble was to fail miserably. As Keegan pulled them in at St James's a foreign player was to be met with almost total disinterest in south east London.

Southampton's tour over, they flew from Amsterdam to the south coast while Keegan flew by himself on a

British Caledonian flight bound for Glasgow via Newcastle. It was a massive newspaper story throughout the country, of course, but on Tyneside it was the equivalent of a Royal visit . . . page one was cleared for the arrival of King Kev.

For an evening newspaper it was a particularly tricky assignment because Newcastle United were determined to say nothing which might take some of the drama out of the Press conference set up for that night. As sports editor of the Evening Chronicle in Newcastle I had an obvious problem. To miss out on Keegan's arrival was unthinkable so in an effort to break the silence I attempted to phone Lawrie McMenemy at his hotel in Holland before the party flew out. Lawrie is a close mate of mine (we both began our soccer education with Gateshead donkey's years ago) and I reckoned he might give me a break. Unfortunately the world and his wife were chasing the Big Man and the nearest I got was to speak to his assistant John Mortimore. I explained the situation but John was unable to help. He had been given instructions that quotes on Keegan were strictly taboo and daren't break the silence.

So I knew nothing bar the fact that it was D-day. I was preparing a speculation piece when the phone rang about ten minutes before edition time and an hour after my negative conversation with Mortimore. When I picked it up, annoyed at being interrupted in full flight, a voice said: 'John? It's Lawrie McMenemy.'

'Who?'

'Lawrie. Listen mate, I haven't got much time. Keegan is flying direct to Newcastle. His plane will arrive at ten to twelve.'

Dear lovely Lawrie. Mortimore had told him that I'd been on the blower trying desperately to speak to him and even though he was about to lose his greatest asset Lawrie felt he owed me a quick call. There he was in Amsterdam Airport shoving the last of his guilders into a coin box while the rest of the Southampton party were checking in. That's the sort of friendship which makes everything worthwhile.

While KK was heading over the North Sea there was one final piece of the jigsaw which had to fall into place — the Football League were threatening not to accept Keegan's registration!

Newcastle still owed around £60,000 of the record £250,000 they had agreed to give West Bromwich Albion for John Trewick in December of 1980 and the League, touchy about clubs reneging on transfer cash, had told United they would not allow any more transfers to go through until West Brom were paid in full. United's directors actually had to dig deep into their own pockets to clear the decks for Keegan.

Once the plane touched down at a cold and blustery Newcastle Airport the mayhem began. For the next six hours until the Gosforth Park Press conference the scene resembled something out of the Keystone Cops.

Newcastle's youth development officer, Brian Watson, drove Arthur Cox's car to the goods exit and, with most of the Press and TV cameras at the main exit, Keegan and his agent were bundled into the back and the car sped off along a perimeter road. The Press gave chase in true pop star fashion and the minutes ticked off as follows:

Twelve-fifteen: Arthur Cox's house in Darras Hall; two o'clock: after speeding down the A1 to Sedgefield a car change saw Cox, Keegan, Watson and Swales joined by a fifth person, United's club doctor Keith Beveridge; 2.10: three miles up the road to the Sedgefield

Community Hospital where Keegan was X-rayed as part of his medical; 3.15: a quick cup of tea at Dr Beveridge's surgery; four o'clock: back along the A1 to the Nuffield Nursing Home in the Jesmond district of Newcastle for further tests; 4.45: return to Cox's home; 6.30: Press conference at the Gosforth Park Hotel.

The words: 'We're in heaven, we've got Kevin' broke United's long silence. Kevin Keegan was a Newcastle United player.

Welcome — a happy Newcastle United fan lifts
Kevin Keegan aloft before his debut game against
QPR.

CHAPTER TWO

Keegan the man

John Toshack and Kevin Keegan were the most famous footballing double act of the seventies. They played up front for Liverpool and were generally accepted as the best attacking partnership in Europe sharing Liverpool's glories up to 1976. People even began to talk about them having a telepathic understanding and they actually took part in a television experiment with limited success.

So when Tosh talks about KK it's obvious that he has inside knowledge of the man.

'Kevin lives the way he plays — unpredictably,' says Toshack. 'If you examine the three moves he has made they all had an element of surprise about them. Why would anyone want to leave Liverpool at the time he went, just after they had won the European Cup for the first time?

'At Hamburg he had done well and overcome the difficult part — he had settled in and become successful. He had done well financially. Why should he have left there for Southampton? Then after finishing top goal-scorer in the First Division with the Saints he leaves for a Second Division club. It doesn't make sense, but it's typical.'

Tosh goes on: 'Keegan has very strong principles — very strong. If, for instance, you upset him that's it. There's no going back. It's not that he's difficult to handle, it's a personal thing, part of his nature. When he makes up his mind it's final. He makes a decision instinctively. It would be no good all of us being like that because as a manager I've had to get the best out of people. But that is his make-up. If you ask any manager he has played for you will be told that little things have happened that they could have done without. Then they will tell you that they had no regrets about signing him.'

Keegan has been accused of being motivated by money, as all top wage earners are accused, but that couldn't be further from the truth.

'A lot of people are just motivated by money in football, but not him,' says Toshack. 'He genuinely needs the constant stimulus of something new and he's brave enough to make decisions on the basis of it. A lot of people would have stayed comfortable at Liverpool or Southampton, but not him.

'Kevin is not frightened of anything . . . he doesn't know the meaning of the word fear. In fact he needs pressure.

'But any team Keegan plays in must accept that he will get preferential treatment from time to time. They must accept that he has earned that right. There must be no petty jealousies or moaning. They must realise that they will all benefit from his presence and ability.'

A lot of footballers believe that when they stop playing their lives are over, but not Keegan. He knows that his life will just be starting when he is finished as a player. He has a young family and will be able to give them so much more of his time. Kevin is a workaholic and inadvertently his wife Jean and the kids must suffer a little as he secures their future through his ability to play football.

One thing is certain: Keegan won't follow the well-worn path of so many famous footballers and become a manager or a coach. His philosophy is that it's hard enough as a player without having your destiny in the hands of eleven other people at three o'clock every Saturday afternoon.

I could see him easily going into public relations, basically selling himself as a personality in the way that Bobby Charlton and former world motor racing champion Jackie Stewart do. They front firms helping sell commodities through their own well-loved public image.

Kevin has done a lot of that on a part-time basis as it is, of course. The Keegan charisma and the business brain of Harry Swales saw KK at his height linked in deals with between fifteen and twenty international companies. That was during his time at Hamburg when he was jetting all over Europe but even when he cut back for family reasons it was still estimated that he earned £250,000 a year from the four companies he was primarily linked with — Fabergé, the Brut people; Patrick Sportswear; Mitre footballs; and Ideal Standard, a shower manufacturing firm in Hull.

'One of the first things to strike me about Kev was his sincerity,' Swales told me. 'I set out to utilize that strength and to develop him as a personality rather than

Kevin Keegan with author John Gibson at one of the many chat shows held throughout the North East.

a footballer. Now he transcends football. Everyone has heard of Kevin Keegan — housewives, schoolgirls, grandmas. He is one of the ten most recognisable faces in Europe.'

Keegan, quite frankly, is the best PR I've ever come across. He's in a class of his own. After joining Newcastle United Kevin worked for Newcastle Breweries doing everything from presenting prizes at leek shows to holding Sunday morning coaching sessions for schoolkids at United's Benwell training ground and doing a series of talk-ins throughout the North East. The breweries used me in a Michael Parkinson-type role on stage with Keegan and it was a privilege to see him work at close range. He's got natural charm and wit, is sometimes too honest for his own good, but generally thinks quickly on his feet to escape particularly difficult questions without offending.

We would do about two hours on stage with Keegan handling even the most intoxicated punters with aplomb and, on occasion, getting one or two of the audience up for a heading competition with him. He always took a load of personal items to give away during the evening and once it was all over he would adjourn to the social club's lounge to set up an autograph session. Keegan would sit there from around ten-thirty until well after midnight not just signing his name but having a few words with every fan and posing for photographs with them. I never saw him once leave a club before the witching hour of twelve midnight.

In that way we raised literally thousands of pounds for the Northumberland Association of Boys' Clubs.

I've done talk-ins with a load of big names such as Brian Clough, Malcolm Macdonald, Lawrie McMenemy, Geoff Boycott, Dennis Lillee, Mike

Brearley, Jack Charlton, Tommy Docherty, Steve Cram and Gareth Edwards. Oh, lots and lots. But not one has done better than Special K.

What's more I can personally vouch for the fact that money is not the god of Keegan. I've done a series of chat shows over the years at Morpeth to raise money for multiple sclerosis research because a mate of mine's wife suffers from the crippling disease. We usually get a sponsor to cover the star name's cash and the 'gate' money goes for research. But Keegan when approached did the show for nothing as long as the point wasn't publicised!

In lots of ways Keegan's image is too good to be true, of course. He reminds me a lot of Cliff Richard inasmuch as he doesn't smoke or drink (apart from a glass of wine with his meal), is handsomely clean-cut and pursued by countless girls without ever falling into the trap of going off the rails, and gives up so much of his private time to his public. However the more you look for a flaw the more you realise that this is the real man and not just a public front.

Mind you, he is human. What Toshack says about the door closing for all time on anyone who dares to cross him, however accidentally, is absolutely true. A lot of people in football, like Bobby Robson, can vouch for that. He quickly makes decisions and sticks by them whether or not they prove to be right.

And he'll have a bet on the horses. He's knowledge-able not only about things like form but about breeding as well — something which his good mate Mike Channon, the former Southampton and England striker, shares with him. At Newcastle Terry McDermott is his constant companion at race meetings all over the country.

29

Says Kevin: 'My dad backed the horses for most of his life and my mum was always onto me, "When you go from here leave the gambling alone. It's a mug's game." I never forgot her advice, which is why I felt uneasy, even guilty and furtive, the first time I went with Mick Channon to Hector Macdonald's, a betting shop near England's West Lodge Park Hotel. But in the end I looked forward to these little excursions. We would joke that Hector had switched his holidays from Butlins to Bermuda the moment he heard that England had picked us again. But we had some good wins as well.'

Keegan received the OBE for his services to football in November 1982. The OBE, it's sometimes said, is won through Other Buggers' Efforts but in Kevin's case it couldn't be farther from the truth. His game is all about effort. He plays as though his life depends on it and it's that hundred per cent commitment which not only makes up for any small deficiencies in his game but inspires other players around him. If my life ever depended on one man I think I'd willingly settle for that man being Kevin Keegan — and there are a lot of footballers who, if they sat next to me in a sinking boat, would encourage me to immediately throw myself overboard!

Kevin's oddball sense of humour earned him a particular nickname in the Liverpool dressing-room . . . Andy MacDaft!

Opposite page: Mike Channon reading his favourite newspaper, the *Sporting Life.*

Old Crazy Horse himself, Emlyn Hughes, says: 'Off the field Kevin is one of my favourite people. Although he is extremely bright, he has such a happy-go-lucky, infectious, slapstick approach to life that he became known as Andy MacDaft. One of his favourite tricks was to come into the dressing-room first thing in the morning clucking like a hen. And he wouldn't stop. There was no conversation; just this infernal squawking which sounded like a hen that had laid an egg.

'He was a very generous fellow and I knew that if ever I felt I needed to talk over a problem he would come to see me on the first available plane out of Hamburg.'

At Newcastle Terry McDermott and Keegan are great practical jokers and once they really caught out chairman Stan Seymour.

Keegan had been linked with the Arabs . . . you know, come and play in Saudi Arabia and there'll be six oil wells at the bottom of your garden. Anyway, Terry Mac dug out the full Arab head dress and robes he had been given in Dubai while on tour with Liverpool and, dressed as a dusky Arab Sheikh, set off for Benwell.

A sharp knock on the manager's door and Arthur Cox was informed that the Arabs were here to talk transfer business over Keegan. Cox thought it was hilarious, joined in, and put through a quick telephone call to St James's asking Stan Seymour and Russell Cushing to stand by. Keegan and the Arab Sheikh would be down immediately. A big transfer was in the offing.

Opposite page: Sheikhing all over — Terry McDermott dressed up and ready to 'bid' for Keegan's transfer.

McDermott and Keegan drove to St James's in Kevin's car — KK33 — with everyone gawping at the Arab sitting in the passenger seat. Russell was peering out of his office window as Terry Mac swept into reception engaged in earnest conversation with Kevin . . . and keeping his head down.

'It was a right hoot,' recalls Terry. 'For a few seconds everyone was fooled. Kevin and Russell introduced me to Mr Seymour who was getting out of his chair to shake me by the hand when I lifted my head dress and winked. It brought the house down.'

Russell Cushing admitted: 'The pair of them had us going for a moment, but McDermott's brown shoes and chip buttie gave him away!'

Supporters in pubs love to tell stories about their heroes and inevitably at Newcastle it's KK and Terry Mac.

The two of them took on the full Sunderland team, or so the story goes. At half time they were 1—0 up when Keegan got a phone call and had to go home to Hampshire. So Terry carried on alone. The next day Keegan phoned to ask how the game had ended.

'We drew 1—1,' said Mac.

'How's that?' asked Kevin. 'We were leading 1—0 when I left.'

'Oh, I know,' replied Terry, 'but I got sent off with ten minutes to go!'

Sitting pretty — that's Kevin on the bonnet of his car, KK33.

Ahoy — Kevin Keegan with members of the
Newcastle crew.

One of the yardsticks of sporting greatness, I've often
felt, is the acceptance of your standing by people outside
your particular domain. Keegan has that.

England Test cricketer Geoff Boycott is someone I've
got to know over the years. He's the least likely person to
fawn over anyone as his record of defiance with York-
shire and England amply demonstrates, but when on the
subject of Keegan he actually glows. 'A real sportsman of
international standing,' was how Boycott summed up
his fellow Yorkshireman to me. 'The man carries himself
with dignity and has the ability when the long knives
come out to just get on with the job. Scoring runs or
scoring goals is the perfect answer to the knockers every
time.'

One of Keegan's many awards on Tyneside —
voted North East Footballer of the Year in 1982.

CHAPTER THREE

Early days

Seventy-four years ago the name Keegan became synonymous with courage and heroism among the mining folk of County Durham. It was in the West Stanley pit disaster of February, 1909 that Frank Keegan's bravery was woven into Geordie folklore. The lives of 168 men and boys were lost but the fact that thirty men and a pit pony survived was entirely due to local inspector Frank Keegan and his rescue team. A poem was written to commemorate the occasion:

Although just rescued from that mine,
Frank Keegan turned again — a rescuer;
He thought not of his own escape from that fiery Hell,
But of his fellow hewer; was such duty ever nobler done?
Was the VC ever nobler won?

Sheer courage has always been the hallmark of the Keegans. Grandfather Frank had it; father Joe had it when he moved his whole family away from Durham's mines when work became scarce; and son Kevin has displayed it time and again on the football fields of the world and in particular in his transfer to a foreign country.

Joe settled his family near Markham Main Colliery where he dug a living for his wife Doris and the kids. It was on February 14, 1951 at Elm Place, Armthorpe that Kevin Keegan was born but it was at 25 Spring Gardens, Doncaster that he was brought up. The place mightn't have been much but at least it had its own gardens, recalled Kevin years later when he saw the Liverpool highrise flats which denied children the right to play in the safety of their own backyards.

Like so many miners Joe suffered from chronic bronchitis and began every day with a massive coughing bout before setting off for the pit. In fact he almost died when Kevin was only nine years old and was forced into a long period of convalescence in Llandudno. The illness prompted Kevin to try and get a job delivering newspapers but he was told he was too small, something which he was to hear repeatedly as he attempted to break into football.

Though his start in the sport was inconspicuous his headmistress at the St Xavier's Roman Catholic School he attended in Doncaster did make mention of his soccer talents in one of his reports. The first 'scout' to catch on, perhaps?

Even so, Kevin's talents at this early stage certainly weren't mind-boggling. He couldn't get into the Doncaster Boys side because of a lad who was a year younger and a better player. His name was Kevin

Pit disaster hero Frank Keegan, grandfather of
Kevin.

Johnson.

'When I thought of him I became a little downhearted because if I was seriously thinking of making it then he had to be a superstar,' said Kevin later. 'Sure enough, he was signed by Sheffield Wednesday and everyone thought he would be a great player but things didn't work out for him.'

Years later Keegan was standing outside Newcastle's ground when Johnson walked up and asked: 'Do you remember me? I'm with Hartlepool now.'

Keegan says: 'There are many obstacles for aspiring footballers from the age of fifteen to eighteen. You can be the best player in the world but might not like living in digs or become too fond of drinking, smoking and women. I'm not saying Kevin Johnson fell foul of these diversions because I don't know, but somewhere along the line, whether it was Sheffield Wednesday's fault or his own, a great young player went astray. It might have been his attitude. He might not have had the nerve or been strong enough. It could have been so many things.

'When you get to First Division level you can have a high degree of skill but something might still be missing. If you're not totally dedicated you'll not make it. The same applies if you have no pace or courage.

'Perhaps Kevin was just an early developer. I am always sceptical when people talk about the best young player I've seen in my life. He might be, but often the worst thing that can happen for the player is to have the fact continually rammed down his throat.'

Academically Keegan didn't pull up any trees, leaving school with 'O' levels in only history and art. Even then jobs weren't easy to come by for lads without qualifications but Kevin got into Peglers Brass Works as a clerk in their central stores. He didn't, however, get straight into their first team at football, being stuck in the reserves for a long time.

Football League clubs looked at Keegan and rejected him. Doncaster Rovers actually gave him the big heave-ho without bothering to look because, having asked for a trial, he turned up late. Coventry City took a month to study him closely and then decided he was too small. What they must feel like today having had England's future captain in their hand and tossed him aside is anyone's guess. One thing's for certain — the bloke who made the decision won't be crowing about it!

It was Scunthorpe United who eventually took the chance — and struck gold. Ron Ashman was the manager at the Old Show Ground. He'd made his name at Norwich City and countless young hopefuls had been through his hands but he remembers Keegan's arrival as though it was yesterday. 'My little diamond,' he calls him.

'It was so simple how it happened,' Ashman told me. 'I had a lad called Bob Nellis who did a bit of scouting for me in the Doncaster area. He played Sunday League soccer and he phoned me to say: "Ron, I've just played against one of the best."

' "Send him over," was my response and Kevin Keegan was on his way. He was a bit weedy and on the small side but he trained with us and I stuck him in our junior team. Jeff Barker, the old Aston Villa and Huddersfield wing-half, ran the Northern Intermediate League team and he came back from Kevin's first game, which was away from home, full of the lad. "We must sign him," Jeff urged. I'd never seen him in a competitive game but when I did I knew immediately that we'd got a little diamond.'

Keegan was sixteen and was to stay with Scunthorpe

until he was nineteen. He signed as an apprentice and played in the juniors and the reserves, who operated in the old North Midlands League.

'Even then he was the leader of the pack,' smiles Ashman. 'He always wanted to be out in front. You know what the little bugger was doing? He was training full time with us and then sneaking off and training with weights to build himself up. We had to stop him.'

Keegan had once done some boxing at the pub-cum-gym in Doncaster where former British heavyweight champion Bruce Woodcock had trained and, having had so many people dismiss him with one quick look at his build, he was determined to overcome any deficiencies as much as possible. He became one of the strongest and most powerfully built players in the Football League, of course.

Keegan's first team debut for Scunthorpe came at the tender age of seventeen. George Kerr, who later became a successful manager at Grimsby Town before moving on to Rotherham United, was injured for an important League Cup tie against the mighty Arsenal and Ashman turned to his young starlet. The date: September 25, 1968.

'I put him in on the right wing and that was the start of things. Arsenal actually wanted to take him on tour with their youth team but UEFA wouldn't allow it because they were playing competitive matches. We'd have let him go for the experience.

'Kevin was in and out of the team at first but soon the buzz was going round that we had a kid who was a bit special. Benny Fenton at Millwall actually offered between £12,000 and £15,000 for Keegan at the age of seventeen but we said "no". We knew it was better to wait. Notts County were in, so were Swindon and West

44

Bromwich Albion — their scout, Paddy Ryan, looked at a striker we had, called Nigel Cassidy, saw Keegan, and began following us all over the place. He knew more about Scunthorpe than any other club.

'Arsenal were also around and they actually said they didn't like his character on the field. Unbelievable, isn't it? Liverpool didn't make their move until the death and by then we needed the money. But Benny Fenton prides himself on being the first in the queue. Whenever I see him he'll say "Remember, I'm the first bloke who offered cash for Keegan." He summed Kevin up quickly.'

Keegan spent three seasons at Scunthorpe making 124 League appearances (four as sub) and scoring eighteen goals. Those figures were topped up by seventeen F.A. Cup and League Cup outings and four more goals.

The breakdown is like this:

1968–69: 29 League games plus four as sub — 3 goals
1969–70: 46 League games — 5 goals
1970–71: 45 League games — 10 goals.

'We played him either on the right wing or in midfield,' said Ashman. 'I remember us going to Colchester and they tried to hammer him. Every time he got the ball he was clattered and I was off the bench once or twice, I can tell you. But it was always like that. Kevin was so quick they couldn't stop him fairly.

'Since he's made the big time I've had one or two people question his skill. What on earth do they want? He can control a ball first time, he thinks and acts quickly, and he can lay it off short or long. And he scores goals. I think the trouble is that his busy style of running deceives some folk. He looks like a runner — a work-horse if you like — but, boy, he can play. He's by far the most outstanding player I've played with or handled in thirty-five years in the game.'

Keegan's old Scunthorpe coach Jack Brownsword was steeped in the club. He was one of that invaluable breed of players whose loyalty is a byword. For twenty-six years Brownsword lived and breathed Scunthorpe, beginning as a non-league player with them in 1946—47, helping them to gain Football League status in 1950, and then reeling off 600 League appearances between 1950 and 1965 which stands to this day as a club record. In all — non-league, League and Cups — Jack pulled on a Scunthorpe shirt 850 times and he didn't join them until the age of twenty-six. When he quit playing he went onto their coaching staff until he sadly parted company with them in January of 1973.

If you want to know about Scunthorpe they say 'ask Jack Brownsword', and if you do he'll tell you: 'In all my time with Scunthorpe we only had one player to match Kevin Keegan for skill.'

That player was Terry Heath, who actually played in the same Scunthorpe team as Keegan and in their last season together (1970—71) was top scorer with eleven goals to Kevin's ten.

'He had been with Leicester and Hull City before he came to us,' Brownsword told me. 'I remember him as a good 'un. He loved the ball on the floor — he could take on people, go past them as though they didn't exist and volley the ball like a dream. He had the lot — bar two things. He didn't have Keegan's temperament and appetite for the game.

'You could look at Terry's face on the team coach going to a match and know that you would get nothing out of him that day. You may as well not play him.

'With Keegan it was different. He had courage and a burning desire to do well. That's why Kevin went all the way and Terry, after getting at cross purposes with Ron Ashman, drifted off to Lincoln.'

Brownsword saw the ambition oozing out of Keegan from the earliest of days.

'The biggest problem was slowing him down,' he said. 'We always had Mondays off after matches but I'd tell Kevin I didn't want to see him until the Wednesday. "Take a couple of days away from training," I'd tell him, "Otherwise you'll burn yourself out."

'When he came at sixteen he was living in digs but by the time he was seventeen he had passed his driving test and got himself a little car so he asked if he could live at home and we said yes. He'd drive the twenty-five miles or so in from Doncaster each morning but he was never late for training. It's better to have a youngster under his own roof if at all possible. I know that Kevin had got homesick during his month at Coventry and we didn't want that interfering with his development.'

In those early days Kevin would often ask Brownsword if he was busy in the afternoons. A 'no' would quickly be followed by a request to do an extra training session after the rest of the Scunthorpe players had finished and gone home. In the close season he took weights home to continue training throughout the summer.

'He arrived looking quite small and light and finished up like a miniature Charles Atlas,' said his coach. 'He became an iron man.'

The Keegan philosophy was 'if you've got a pair of boots let's play football'.

Brownsword recalls: 'If there was a junior match in midweek Kevin would be the first to volunteer to play. Once he played for the first team in Wales on the Tuesday night and then asked if he could report straight back to Scunthorpe to play for the reserves on the Wednesday.

'He'd even round up players for you. We were playing a junior match at Sheffield one Saturday and had to pick up four players in Doncaster en route. When we got there only two were waiting. There wasn't a sign of the other two so we couldn't field a full team. "Don't worry," said Keegan. "I'll get you a couple of players." He directed the bus to the street where he used to live and knocked on the door of two of his mates. One was actually still in bed but they both came trooping out with their boots and on we went to Sheffield with a full complement.'

Only once did Brownsword see another side of Keegan and that, too, was in a junior match. Kevin had turned up casually dressed and Jack pulled him to one side to point out that club policy was to wear a collar and tie on match days. The response was totally unexpected.

'Oh, get stuffed,' snapped Keegan.

'That was very, very unlike Kevin and it was obvious that he was upset,' recalls Jack. 'I took him into the medical room for a private talk but still it didn't lift him out of his depression. The opposition ran all over us in the first half and Keegan was doing nothing.

'At half time I got hold of him again. I gave him a right going over and told him that he could beat this lot on his own if he wanted. Something must have got through to him because he turned it on in the second half. He threw petrol on the game; set it alight. And we won.'

Jack used to partner Kevin at cards on the team bus and on the golf course and the attitude was always the same: 'He had to win. Even if we went out on road runs it was the same. We'd start at 10 a.m. and the bulk of us would end up back at the ground at about noon. But by then Kevin had been in, showered and changed, and was having a cup of coffee down the street.'

Liverpool got Keegan for a mere £35,000. Bill Shankly called it 'robbery without violence' and there's no question that it was. But then hasn't Keegan always been cheap? His move to Hamburg was for £500,000 and then, because he began fixing his own fee, Southampton paid £400,000 and Newcastle United £100,000. Compare that with the £1m Manchester City paid for both Steve Daley and Kevin Reeves plus the three £1m transfers of Trevor Francis to Nottingham Forest, Manchester City and Sampdoria as well as Luther Blissett's £1m departure to Italy, and Keegan looks a snip.

Kevin looks back on his transfer to Liverpool with a twinkle in his eye.

'My dad always said to me, "Don't undersell yourself, son," so when Bill Shankly offered me £40 a week or whatever I replied, "That's not good enough. I think I deserve more." Out of the corner of my eye I could see Ron Ashman sinking to the floor. Scunthorpe desperately needed the money and the deal was going down the pan in front of his very eyes. Shanks thought for a moment and then said: "All right, then. How about £45?" "Done," I said, quick as a flash. Really I was dying to sign for Liverpool.'

Ashman insists that Keegan hasn't changed since the day he walked into the Old Show Ground.

'He's just the same sort of bloke — success hasn't gone to his head,' said Ron. 'When I got the sack from my last managerial job I decided to seek a bit more security at my time of life. I went into insurance for six months and then decided to open a travel shop in Scunthorpe High Street. Around that time, season '82-'83, I went to Elland Road to see Keegan play for Newcastle against Leeds in the Milk Cup. I knew Arthur Cox and Tommy Cavanagh and we were talking with Kevin. I told them of my plans and straight away Kevin said, "I know you want Barry Manilow but I'll open your shop for you." He did, too, and what's more he didn't charge a penny.'

Joe Keegan was a proud father as his son Kevin came through the ranks to Liverpool. He was also proud of his Geordie heritage and had got to know the great Jackie Milburn, who was centre-forward for Newcastle United and England in the fifties.

'I met Joe after a match at St James's and we talked a lot about Newcastle United and the pits,' said Jackie. 'We had both things in common. Joe supported Newcastle and I'd been in the pits before becoming a footballer. After that we exchanged letters quite a bit . . . they were always full of gossip about the old days and the mines.

'When Kevin first came up to St James's with Liverpool Joe introduced us. "This is my lad," he said proudly. He really glowed when talking about Kevin and so he should. I only wish he'd lived to see Kevin play for Newcastle United. That would have been his crowning glory.'

Opposite page: Jackie Milburn, who wrote regularly to Kevin's father Joe Keegan.

CHAPTER FOUR

Anfield glories

KEEGAN ARRIVED AT ANFIELD IN THE spring of 1971 and departed after Liverpool had won the European Cup for the first time in the spring of 1977. In between Keegan and Liverpool plundered soccer's greatest trophies with monotonous regularity — the Football League championship, the F.A. Cup, the UEFA Cup and the European Cup all became theirs while Keegan was also voted Footballer of the Year.

It was a partnership of passion, a fusion of two great talents. And out of it came a love which has remained unabated to this very day. Bill Shankly, the man who signed Keegan for Liverpool, will never be replaced in his affections.

Despite his rise to fame at Anfield Keegan wasn't exactly unknown when Shanks signed him. Several clubs had noted his displays in the Fourth Division and some people had marked him down as potentially a great player. The question was: how quickly could he make the transition to the big time?

Shanks dispatched his trusted right-hand men, Bob Paisley and Joe Fagan, to Scunthorpe for the final verdict. Andy Beattie had sworn that Keegan would make it but Liverpool had to judge for themselves.

Paisley recalls: 'We watched Kevin, who was skippering the side, for twenty minutes then we headed for home. When Shanks asked, "What about him?" The answer was, "Take him." '

The reasoning was that Keegan would be a replacement for Ian Callaghan who, at that time, was struggling after a cartilage operation. Instead, Cally recovered both fitness and form and played another six years at the top!

The day before the League season opened Shanks called Kevin into his office and asked him where he wanted to play. Kevin replied: 'Home to Nottingham Forest, boss, in the first team.' Shankly pushed Keegan up front, and a game later moved Callaghan to the centre of midfield. Both moves came off. After fourteen minutes of his debut match Keegan scored from a John Toshack pass, Liverpool won 3—1, and the show was on the road.

'Kevin fully justified the chance Shanks took on him as a front runner,' said Paisley later. 'At Scunthorpe he had been playing on the right side of midfield and detesting it. We'd noticed that he always seemed to be veering to the left and that was another bonus for most players are naturally right-sided and when you get a genuine left-sided footballer he helps to give a team all-round balance.

'In fact although we had earmarked him for the right-sided midfield job Ian Callaghan had been doing we came to realise after a time that there was no way Kevin

A youthful looking Kevin Keegan, pictured just
after joining Liverpool in 1971.

would have replaced Cally there. As time went on he built up a formidable striking partnership with John Toshack and, with no disrespect to Tosh, I have to say that Kevin was the major partner. John had the brains and the aerial ability but his mobility was limited. Tosh got into positions, Kevin made up the ground by his speed and stamina.'

Keegan was to quickly learn the wisdom of the incredible Shanks, a legend amongst managers. He's often told me the following tale:

'Early on in my first season we were playing West Ham at Anfield and I was up against England's World Cup captain Bobby Moore, a giant of a player. Shanks knew it and before the kick-off he came bounding into our dressing-room and over to me. "Son," he said. "I've just seen that Bobby Moore come in. He's been in the nightclubs again, son. He's got baggy eyes, and he's limping. He looks awful, son, you'll massacre him." By the time we were ready to go out I felt I was playing against an old, one-legged geriatric.

'In those days West Ham were renowned for playing you off the park and losing 5—0. And, basically, that's the way it went. Moore was immaculate but we still won and I managed to score.

'After the game Shanks made a point of wandering across to me. "Jesus Christ, son," he said. "You'll never play against a fitter or better player than Bobby Moore. He's a master!"

'It was Shanks' way of lifting a player before a match and then bringing him down to earth.'

In Keegan's first season Liverpool failed to win the First Division championship by a solitary point but next time round — 1972—73 — was the most successful in the club's history to date. Not only did Liverpool win the

League title, but, after playing in Europe for almost a decade, they were rewarded with their first European trophy, the UEFA Cup.

The fearsome partnership of Keegan and Toshack powered Liverpool to the Division One championship with sixty points, three ahead of Arsenal. Kevin scored fourteen goals in forty-one League games and Tosh thirteen in twenty-one appearances.

Ironically in view of what was to come Liverpool beat the crack West German club Borussia Monchengladbach in the two-legged UEFA final thanks to two goals from Keegan. And a little bit of Shanks' luck!

Tosh in his autobiography writes: 'The home leg was to be played on the Wednesday night before the home internationals and I had been included in the Welsh squad whose first game was at Wrexham against Scotland. Shanks picked his side and I was one of five substitutes. Although the first leg was at home, Liverpool were going to play with just two forwards, Keegan and Heighway.

'The Germans had spoken of their intention to attack but when the game began the great midfield player Gunter Netzer was playing as a sweeper. For twenty minutes the Germans contained us without too much bother but then a freak rainstorm caused the match to be abandoned and it was decided to replay the game the following night. I came into Anfield the following morning and went to see Shanks. The conversation went something like this: "Hello, John, son, how are you?"

' "Not very well, actually."

' "Oh, I'm sorry to hear that."

' "I'll tell you what, boss, you must be the luckiest man alive. You've gone out at home in a European final playing with two men up because the Germans kidded you into believing they would attack. Who picks the team here — you, or Paisley and Fagan?"

'With that Shanks blew his top. "Get out of here, who the hell do you think you are talking to?"

' "You can stuff your team," I retorted, "You'll be lucky to get a corner tonight."

'With that Shanks walked out and slammed the door. I drove home to Formby wondering which club I would be playing for next season. I had arrived home and was just telling my wife Sue what had happened when the telephone rang. "Hello, son, are you not in bed yet?"

' "No, boss, I've only just got home."

' "Well, you get to your bed, there is a good chance you will be playing tonight." I knew then I was in the side.

'When we all arrived at the ground Shanks closed the dressing-room door and said, "Boys, I am going to make one change from last night's side. John will replace Brian Hall." Bob and Joe looked down to the floor. Poor Brian Hall was shocked.

'The game ended in a 3—0 win for us with goals from Keegan (2) and Larry Lloyd. I caused havoc in the air and was instrumental in our victory. After the game Shanks told the Press that he had spotted a weakness the night before and had brought me in to exploit it. The reporters hailed it as a piece of Shankly brilliance but I think that but for that blazing row in the morning I would not have played.'

Opposite page: Newcastle United full-back Alan Kennedy jumps above Liverpool's Kevin Keegan during the 1974 F.A. Cup final at Wembley.

Liverpool took the UEFA Cup with them to West Germany for the return leg (Spurs had been the previous holders) but they had to endure forty-five minutes of sheer brilliance before the cup was theirs. Borussia's midfield of Wimmer, Danner and Netzer tore them to shreds and Heynckes scored twice to make the aggregate score 3—2 to Liverpool at half-time.

Shanks dug deep to try and kid Liverpool through. He told them the Germans had shot their bolt and then, when the waves began to pound the rocks again, he was up on his feet telling the ref to look at his watch. But hold on Liverpool did to gain the first of their many European successes after a European Cup semi-final, a Fairs Cup semi-final and a Cupwinners' Cup final.

Almost unbelievably Bill Shankly was to retire at the end of the following season, in 1974, when Liverpool won the F.A. Cup at Wembley defeating Newcastle United 3—0 in a terribly one-sided game.

Keegan was to star, too, against one of his future clubs.

In those days my job was to travel with Newcastle United for my newspaper. The path to the final had been spectacular for the Geordies as they won through every round away from home with their hordes of noisy supporters sending the Blaydon Races reverberating round every stadium and their beloved Super Mac, Malcolm Macdonald, scoring in every round. But even I was uneasy about the final itself. The Liverpool machine was awesome and I always remember doing a telly inter-view in Wembley week for the local ITV network in which I named Keegan and Steve Heighway as the two men who could break Geordie hearts. It was to prove chillingly correct.

Shanks stole a march as only he could on the morning of the final. The TV cameras moved into the teams'

Not this time — Newcastle United goalkeeper Iam
McFaul gathers a cross in the '74 final watched by
Keegan (centre) and Newcastle skipper Bob Moncur.

hotels and the players gathered round and answered
questions about the impending match through their
captains, Emlyn Hughes and Bob Moncur. As the interviews drew to a close and the Liverpool party were being
faded out Bill Shankly chipped in quickly with a remark
he hoped the Newcastle players would overhear.

'Did you hear that, boys?' he said. 'They looked frightened to death.'

Liverpool had won the war of words and gained a
telling psychological point.

Steve Heighway, one of Liverpool's scorers in the defeat of Newcastle United, leaves Bob Moncur in his wake.

It's a goal — Keegan (No. 7) turns away after
scoring Liverpool's third goal in the '74 Cup final.

Newcastle hung on till half-time without ever threatening to ruffle the Liverpool back four. Then the flood-
gates opened. Alec Lindsay 'scored' after a sweet one-
two with Keegan only for referee Gordon Kew to rule it
offside, but in fifty-seven minutes the darting, dynamic
Keegan struck. A Heighway throw-in on the right was
picked up by Smith and he hit a low cross that Hall
dummied to allow Keegan to bring it under control and
beat McFaul with a fierce half volley: 1—0.

Seventy-seven minutes and it was Heighway's turn.
Clemence kicked long and Toshack nudged it on for
Heighway to take the ball in space and drive it home
with his right foot: 2—0.

Newcastle, in disarray and with their sub on, would have settled for escaping at that but with two minutes to go Keegan finished off the massacre after Smith had crossed from the right: 3—0.

Keegan was unquestionably the man of the match with the top Newcastle performance on a shoddy day being turned in by Terry McDermott. A Kopite as a kid, McDermott was soon to link up with Keegan at Liverpool and they were to play in the same England side together. What's more, by 1982 they had both gone the full circle and were wearing the black and white of Newcastle trying to breathe new life into a distinguished club.

As Shanks left Wembley's hallowed turf two exuberant Liverpool fans who had broken though the security raced up to him, dropped on their knees and literally kissed his feet. No one, bar probably Bill himself, knew at that moment that we were saying goodbye to a footballing Picasso. A few months later, on July 12, 1974, Bill announced his retirement and seven years later, in the early hours of September 29, 1981, he died.

Shanks' job went to his lieutenant Bob Paisley — much to the surprise of Keegan and, he claims, most of the Liverpool players.

Kevin told me: 'We honestly thought that Bob was a stop-gap. Someone to hold the fort before a big name appeared. He had been Shanks' hatchet man doing the dirty jobs around the place . . . you know, the unpleasant jobs with players that the boss didn't want to do himself.

'I'll always remember the day he was made manager. We were all standing around the dressing room in our Melwood training ground when in came Bob. He walked over, put his back against the wall, and said:

Happy days — the Liverpool team show off the
F.A. Cup after their 1974 triumph.

"Eeeee, I never wanted the job anyway!" in that Geordie
twang of his. He looked positively embarrassed.

'But it shows how wrong you can be because Bob
Paisley went on to become the most successful manager
in the history of the game. His record is magnificent.'

The blackest period of Keegan's career was about to
unfold and it had nothing to do with the managerial
change at Anfield.

As Cup winners Liverpool went to Wembley for the
showpiece Charity Shield match which unfolds every
brand new season. But this time instead of it being a

splendid spectacle fit to lay before a million people it was niggly, bad-tempered and downright ugly. A terrible advert for our national sport. One of the problems, no doubt, was the fact that Liverpool's opponents were their arch rivals Leeds United. At that time Liverpool and Leeds were the giants of the First Division and, in their joint quest for glory, a fierce competitiveness had been built up between the two clubs. Even an open dislike.

Anyway, the game was marred by fouls and exploded in the second half, culminating in the infamous sending off of Keegan and Billy Bremner, the first British players to be sent off at Wembley. And to add to the disgrace, you might remember, both players threw their shirts down on the touchline.

But let's look back at the whole picture through the eyes of people who were there.

Tommy Smith in his book *I Did It The Hard Way* recalls: 'The Charity Shield game was a bit of a shambles — Bremner and Keegan were sent off and I got booked along with Johnny Giles. As soon as we started the game Allan Clarke went over the ball to Phil Thompson and when I say went over the ball he could have broken his leg. But he wasn't pulled up for it. Then later in the first half I went in on Clarke hard and I got booked. So by half-time there was more than a bit of needle in the game.'

Opposite page: Liverpool skipper Emlyn Hughes lifts the European Cup aloft after their stunning win in Rome. Behind him is Jimmy Case.

Paisley takes up the story: 'Johnny Giles had already been booked for clouting Kevin Keegan before Billy Bremner and Kevin got involved in another incident in the second half when the two players swapped punches. Referee Bob Matthewson ordered them both off and they both threw their shirts down on the ground.

'I'm still the last person to condone that sort of behaviour but at the same time I still believe the two players were victims of circumstance and that those who sit in judgement were unjustified in coming down on them like a ton of bricks.'

For Keegan it was a nightmare ... his second dismissal in five days after being sent off in a friendly against Kaiserslautern in West Germany.

The fact that Giles had been booked for hammering him and Bremner had similarly fouled him before he retaliated was of little consolation to Keegan. He received an automatic three-match ban for being sent off and was then charged with bringing the game into disrepute which brought a further eight-match sentence and a fine of £500. That meant in total he was to miss no fewer than eleven games.

The case of Keegan and Bremner had come at a time when soccer hooliganism was bang in the headlines — a fan had been stabbed to death at Blackpool the previous weekend. There was a clamour for two of football's biggest names to be made an example of and there was actually direct Home Office pressure brought to bear as the F.A. Disciplinary Committee sat in judgement.

It was a testing first season for Paisley. He lost his star player for eleven matches; inherited Ray Kennedy, a striker Shanks had bought on the day he retired; saw the transfer of John Toshack to Leicester fall through on medical grounds; and, a month after selling Larry Lloyd

68

to Coventry, lost his replacement, Phil Thompson, through a cartilage operation. All the same Liverpool finished runners-up in the League championship two points behind Derby County and the foundations were laid for what was to come — the League and UEFA Cup double in 1975—76 and the League and European Cup double in 1976—77 before Keegan left.

One of Paisley's problems which had to be sorted out immediately was his striking partnership. When Kennedy was signed for £200,000 and Tosh was struggling with injuries it seemed that was that. Especially when Leicester came in for Tosh. But the deal collapsed and by the end of the season the big Welshman was firmly established again alongside Keegan.

Paisley was to brilliantly solve the Kennedy poser. Ray had been Arsenal's top scorer when they did the double in 1971 and he was bought by Shanks as an out-and-out centre-forward. But when the big Geordie found it hard to settle into the Liverpool pattern Paisely heard a whisper from a North East schoolteacher that Kennedy used to play midfield as a kid. So the experiment was tried out in the reserves and it exceeded even Bob's wildest expectations. Kennedy went on to become a vital cog in Liverpool's machine and an England international.

A very good pal of mine, Ray has often told me of the sheer panic as, while driving through the Liverpool streets by taxi on his way to sign for the club, he saw huge billboards proclaiming: 'Bill Shankly quits.'

It could have all gone so wrong for him — a new manager on the day he signed. What if Paisley didn't rate him? Or if he didn't like Paisley?

Instead it was to be the making of the man and

Kennedy still rates Paisley as the cream of the crop.

The 1976 League championship was clinched in the last match at Molineux when Liverpool had to win or draw to pip QPR for the title and Wolves had to win to stay up. With only quarter of an hour to go Liverpool were trailing to a Steve Kindon goal when Keegan struck oil. A Tommy Smith centre was headed on by Tosh at the near post and there was Keegan to bury the ball and, with it, Wolves' hopes of escaping the hangman's noose. All the anxieties drained away from Liverpool's play and the championship was clinched in style with further goals from Toshack and Ray Kennedy.

The value of Keegan to Liverpool was underlined at Molineux and rammed home again a fortnight later when his personal rescue act produced the Second League and UEFA Cup double in three years.

Bruges proved to be awkward European opponents. In their first leg of the UEFA final at Anfield two early goals and a well rehearsed offside trap had Liverpool under the cosh but they managed to nose in front 3—2. Then in the critical return in Belgium Tommy Smith conceded a penalty in the first ten minutes which centre-forward Raoul Lambert tucked away.

The teams were tied 3—3 on aggregate but a swerving free-kick from Keegan unlocked the door and the Cup was Liverpool's.

Kevin Keegan stood at the pinnacle of English football, the man of the moment. Apart from a First Division championship medal and a European winner's medal he had already had the honour of captaining England and was voted Footballer of the Year.

Though a few imitations have sprung up over the years this award from the Football Writers' Association is the one that really matters. It's the traditional one

Liverpool's anthem . . . you'll never walk alone.

dating back thirty-six years to when Stanley Matthews became the first winner in 1948. Keegan's name went on the roll of honour alongside such other greats as Matthews, Johnny Carey, Joe Mercer, Billy Wright, Tom Finney, Danny Blanchflower, Bobby Moore, Bobby Charlton, George Best and Billy Bremner. I'm glad to say that my humble vote went to Keegan in 1976.

Kevin's last season in the blood red shirt of Liverpool will be remembered as the one when the mightiest club in the land almost pulled off the unbelievable treble. Liverpool won the First Division Championship and the European Cup but lost to Tommy Docherty's Manchester United in the F.A. Cup final at Wembley.

But it was also to be a season when Keegan rarely showed the form he was capable of though his finale in Rome was to be as spectacular as any bonfire night fireworks celebration.

71

The reason for Keegan's patchy play was that the Continentals were beginning to take an interest in England's little jack-in-the-box and Kevin himself felt ready for a new challenge.

Being an honest lad, Keegan admitted publicly that he was ready to go abroad and, quite naturally, the Press, radio and television were full of it. That was a mistake, as Kevin now admits.

He told me: 'If I could have my time over again I would never have announced publicly that I was going at the end of the season. It brought untold pressures. If I had a good game some of the fans would say it was because I was playing to get away and if I had a bad 'un it was because I didn't care as I was going.'

Barcelona were the early front runners for Keegan then Real Madrid offered £650,000 for him but Kevin was anxious to have a crack at the European Cup with Liverpool before leaving and so the Spaniards missed out.

The speculation and the pressure mounted and for the first time in his life he was at loggerheads with a section of the Anfield crowd who were angry that they were about to lose the greatest player in the country, a player they literally worshipped.

To make matters worse Kevin's father Joe died in the December. They had been very close and the tragedy hurt Kevin deeply. Nevertheless Liverpool won the first Division championship and Keegan finished top scorer with twelve goals — and the F.A. Cup final and European Cup final were still to come.

Looking back immediately after his £500,000 transfer to Hamburg, Keegan went on record as saying: 'I'd love to turn the clock back to before Christmas and play some of those games again. I don't think I did myself justice. I was very despondent about the whole thing and I seemed to lose interest in the things around me. If the Hamburg deal hadn't gone through I was seriously thinking of packing in the game and concentrating on my future in business. It may sound terrible but I was getting more pleasure out of my outside interests than I was from my football.

'It got to such a stage that I said to my wife Jean that if a foreign club came in for me but insisted that I signed there and then before the F.A. Cup final and the European Cup final I would have gone. It was some days before she realised that I wasn't joking.'

The F.A. Cup final at Wembley was the killer because that was where the treble was sacrificed. I was in my usual seat in the Press box and, frankly, I thought that Manchester United were lucky to win 2—1. Liverpool played well and scored the best goal of the match through Jimmy Case. And United's winner was a sheer fluke — Lou Macari's shot was going wide when it hit Jimmy Greenhoff on the chest and was deflected into the net.

Keegan played indifferently and Paisley has told me since: 'That was the difference. If Kevin had played well we would have probably won the Cup but, then, if Wembley had been his platform would he have been able to play so magnificently in Rome five days later?'

Rome, indeed, was the crowning glory. Liverpool beat Borussia Monchengladbach 3—1 in the Olympic Stadium with Keegan giving due warning to all West Germans that he was on his way with a display out of the very top drawer. That victory was, without a doubt, the best of Liverpool's three European Cup wins.

In West Gemany they love the rigid man-for-man marking system and in Rome Borussia put the great

Training's over and Liverpool coach Ronnie Moran
and manager Joe Fagan clear away.

Berti Vogts on Keegan. Vogts followed Kevin everywhere. He was like a second skin but all to no avail. The
German was led a dog's life and Tosh, who missed the
final through injury, declared: 'Kevin's performance
that day was the main reason we won the European
Cup.'

Paisley called the opening goal 'a coaching showpiece.' Keegan pulled Vogts away to the touchline as
Callaghan won the ball in midfield and pushed it out to
Heighway on the right. Cally followed on down the
flank, pulling the Germans even wider and allowing
Heighway to cut inside and play the ball into McDermott's path. Terry's anticipation and off-the-ball

74

running had been exploited to the full and he gleefully drove home a low shot.

McDermott must have covered fifty yards in that move — a typical Liverpool goal.

The score was unchanged into the second half until Liverpool made their first mistake and were punished for it. They lost the ball ten yards outside their own penalty area and Allan Simonsen flashed a whiplash shot across Clemence and into the far corner of the net. Would all their brilliance be blown away with the Germans stealing the trophy? The answer was an emphatic 'no' courtesy of Tommy Smith. A Heighway corner on the left saw the teak-hard Smith arrive late to power a header beyond the grasping fingers of Kneib. Tommy was normally the saver of games not the winner but every dog has its day and that moment belonged to him.

The West Germans were sagging and when Keegan went on another of his lung-bursting runs Vogts chased him with despair from the right touchline into the Monchengladbach penalty area and pulled him down. Penalty! Up stepped Phil Neal to take it and he admits: 'It was almost too much for me to pick up the ball and put it on the spot.

'I knew if I scored they would be dead and if I missed it would give them the momentum to get right back in the game. I remember looking at their goalkeeper and thinking he must be 6ft 4in tall. He blocked out the entire goal. I'd taken a penalty in the semi-final in Zurich and hit it to the goalkeeper's left so I decided to hit this one to the other side. The keeper must have studied that particular kick on television because he dived the wrong way. It was the most important single kick of my career — and there was that lovely ball in the back of the net. It was a glorious moment.

'I've seen so many pictures of that goal but my favourite is the one that shows Ian Callaghan behind me with his hands together as though he is praying. He'd won everything in football apart from a European Cup medal and it was as though he was saying, "Go on Phil, stick it in and finish it off." I was glad to do it for him.'

Keegan, hustling and tackling, passing and running, was now the talk of Europe after his performance which was described as the most complete individual performance ever alongside Stanley Matthews in the 1953 Cup final, Alfredo di Stefano in the 1960 European Cup final and Pele during the 1970 World Cup.

Said Keegan: 'I think it was one of my very best games when you take into consideration the occasion, the fact that I was playing against Berti Vogts, and that people had come to see what I was worth.'

That game cemented a special relationship that Keegan now has with Vogts. 'I consider him the greatest professional I've ever played against,' said Keegan. 'He's one of the nicest men in football. If everyone in football, or in life, were like him it would be a better world to live in.

'After that final in Rome Berti went back to his hotel and must have been right down in the dumps. After all, he's never won a European Cup medal and now I'd given him a difficult night and made him give away a penalty. But later on that night he came across to our hotel to have a celebration drink with me. I could never have done it. I wish I could but I'm a very bad loser. For me there is only one thing — winning.'

Opposite page: Bobby Moore . . . set up by Bill Shankly at Anfield.

CHAPTER FIVE

Shanks . . . and others

'THE MOST POWERFUL INFLUENCE ON MY career was a manager. I owe my England caps to Bill Shankly of Scotland. He signed me for Liverpool, opened my eyes, made me a player; he was the first to instil into me the idea of targets. "Jesus Christ," he was always saying, "you're a great player. You're not just a great player, you're one of *the* great players."

'Shankly gave me something to prove; I started becoming a good player because he swore that I was one. When others joined the chorus I found something within my armoury that helped me do justice to their assessments. I can motivate myself now, but as a fresh kid from a small club I needed someone to believe in me. Shankly was the man; if I had gone to another manager I probably wouldn't be where I am today.'

That tribute to Shanks was paid by Kevin Keegan himself in his book *Against the World.*

Bill was a colourful character. His close cropped hair, his machine gun words and defiant stance made him a ringer for James Cagney. He loved the gangsters of the prohibition days and the fight game but beneath it all he was staunchly patriotic. If Shanks ever varied from his motto 'British is best' it was only to say 'Liverpool is best'.

He established a unique rapport with the Anfield crowd and with his players. The KGB would have loved him as a brain-washer — he used to make the players feel like giants and opponents almost like pygmies.

So many stories have grown up around Shanks that it's difficult to tell fact from fiction. His flair with words, his ability to turn a phrase and sometimes accidentally bring about the funniest of lines, have become legend.

We've all heard the Shanks one liners: 'There are only two teams in Liverpool — Liverpool and Liverpool Reserves'; and 'Football isn't life and death, it's more serious than that.' Then there's the popular after-dinner story that when Nessie, his wife, complained of never going out Bill took her to watch Accrington Stanley as a birthday treat.

Whether that's true is open to debate but there are a few absolutely true Shanks tales which Keegan loved to tell when we did our chat shows.

Like the time when the Anfield backroom staff of Shanks, Reuben Bennett, Bob Paisley, Joe Fagan and Ronnie Moran were playing the apprentices in a five-a-side.

Training was finished for the day but still this game was going on and a few of the senior players, mugs of tea in their hands, drifted out to watch. Shanks' team was obviously struggling and one of the kids went round Reuben to clip a shot inside the near post. 'No goal, no

Bill Shankly and his beloved Kop.

goal. It was too high,' yelled Shankly. There were posts about three foot high but no crossbar and the arguements went on and on. Eventually Shanks decided to call in Chris Lawler, who was watching, to act as arbiter.

'Here, Chris, was that a goal or not?' he said.

Lawler shuffled his feet uncomfortably and coughed. 'Well, boss, I think it just crept in under the bar,' he murmured.

Shanks went purple. 'Jesus Christ, son,' he exploded. 'You've been here twelve years and never said a word. And now the first time you open your mouth you tell a bloody lie!'

Then there was the occasion when Liverpool signed Ron Yeats, a colossus of a man. Yeats was stripped and in the shower when Shanks held an impromptu Press conference.

'Look at him, come on, look at him,' waxed Shankly. 'Isn't he magnificent? Come on, boys, see for yourself.' And at that half a dozen Press men solemnly walked round Yeats admiring his superb build as the shower cascaded down on all of them.

Early in Liverpool's European days Yeats skippered them abroad and the team got beaten. Shanks couldn't understand it and walked round the dressing-room scratching his head. Then he walked over to Yeats.

'Tell me, son, what did you call at the toss up?' he enquired.

'Heads, boss,' came the reply.

'Aye, I knew it. You should have called tails,' growled Shanks.

Bill had an answer for everything even on the rare occasion a player didn't want to join Liverpool.

Lou Macari was a Scottish international with Glasgow Celtic and Shanks wanted to sign him. Lou went down to Liverpool, agreed terms, and all that was left was the formality of his signature on the transfer forms. A proud Shanks even took him into the dressing-room and introduced him as a new colleague. Macari said that in fairness he felt obliged to talk to Manchester United since they, too, had expressed an interest in him. The following morning the papers were full of Macari signing for Tommy Doc and, not unnaturally, the Anfield dressing-room buzzed with the news as the players prepared for training. When Shanks walked in he saw the papers lying in the middle of the room with the Macari headlines a foot high.

Opposite page: Lou Macari — he turned down Shanks.

'Hell's bells, boys, I only wanted him for our reserve team,' he snarled. 'He couldnae play anyway.'

No manager was more loyal to his players and if anyone dared to criticize them outside of himself he'd go in all guns firing. Even if it was someone at Anfield. Shankly, no respecter of persons anyway, was really annoyed with one director's vociferous criticisms of a Liverpool player who was having a real off day. His comments needled Shanks who charged into the board-room after the game and ranted: 'Did you hear that stupid so-and-so . . .?' When somebody pointed out that the fellow he was slating was standing behind him Shanks wheeled round, looked him in the eye, and said: 'Aye, that's the bugger!'

Malcolm Macdonald — old Super Mac himself — found the same biting comment when he had a go at Shankly's much-loved club. Newcastle United were playing at Liverpool and Macdonald, always one for the patter, saw the sign 'This is Anfield' above the tunnel. Turning to Joe Harvey he said: 'I see we've come to the right place then.'

'Aye,' growled Shanks, 'ya have. And you'll find out when you get out there.' They did, too. Newcastle were slaughtered.

His love of gangster films and the wild west saw Bill arrive in New York, jump in a taxi, and demand: 'Take me to Boot Hill.' He actually thought there was such a place!

But for all his passions Shanks never took to America. When he went over there to meet the rest of the Liver-

Opposite page: The sign Malcolm Macdonald scoffed — and lived to rue the day!

pool party in their New York hotel Bob Paisley asked him if he'd like to visit Jack Dempsey's bar. He looked at his watch and said no, it was too late.

'But it's only half-past six,' said Paisley.

'It bloody well isn't,' rapped Shanks. 'It's half past eleven. No Yank is going to tell me what time it is.'

Bill had refused to alter his watch after leaving England and he was to keep it on English time for the rest of the tour.

A story handed down from the older Liverpool players concerns their first trip in the European Cup. They were on their way to the Icelandic capital of Reykjavik when the plane was held up at Prestwick due to fog. With time to kill Shanks decided to take the party round a whisky distillery but they got lost on the narrow fog-bound lanes. Eventually Shanks, who was sitting next to the door, yanked it open and called to a cyclist: 'Excuse me, we are Liverpool and we're on our way to Reykjavik.'

Before he could utter another word the cyclist replied: 'I think you're on the wrong road, pal.'

Shanks' face was a picture.

Bob Paisley once beautifully summed up the difference between himself and Shanks when we were talking about the difficulty of following such a popular man.

'Bill used to like to wear steel caps on his shoes so you could hear him coming a mile away,' said Paisley. 'Me, I prefer rubber soles!'

That softly, softly approach was to strike a rich vein as Liverpool went from success to success.

In the old days Paisley had acted as a buffer between Shanks and the players. Keegan told me: 'If the boss wanted to play a certain player on the Saturday or leave another out the job of breaking the news was given to Bob. Often he would come into the treatment room and

Two Liverpool stalwarts — Emlyn Hughes and
Tommy Smith.

walk over to, say, the bloke lying next to me. The lad
would have just been telling me how the injury was
coming along nicely but Bob would take a sharp intake
of breath, shake his head, and say: "We'd better give it
another week." Then he'd come over to me, glance at my
leg, and declare: "Looks good, Kevin. Should be all right
for Saturday." And I'd probably have a broken leg!'

As a manager Paisley assumed full responsibility. His
deep knowledge of the game and his ability to be ruthless
when required drove Liverpool on. He may look like
everyone's favourite uncle with his woolly Marks and
Sparks cardigans three sizes too big and his Brylcreemed

hair but Paisley could do what was necessary. His tactics were sound but to the uninitiated they were probably undecipherable. The reason was his Geordie twang. Kevin elaborates: 'Bob's team talks were choice. He'd often use different names for players: "if you pick up thingymebob and then Phil can close down on whatshisname," he'd say and we'd all understand.

'It was worse on occasions. When we played Newcastle United they had a winger called Stewart Barrowclough and Bob would say things like, "watch that fellow Wheelbarrow, he's fast." On another occasion he pinpointed an opponent and said, "now this fellow — he's not very fast but he's nippy." '

Despite Paisley's quaint sayings and the lighthearted laughs there was a deep respect brought about by results. Bob followed the greatest act in the world and topped it.

His humour was there, all right. In his office, hardly big enough to swing a cat, he had a clock above his desk which went backwards and a poster of a litter of pigs scrambling over their mother with a caption that read: 'It isn't easy to stay on top.'

But listen to the man and his words are 22-carat gold. I once spent three days at his elbow and learned the lessons of a lifetime. Bob lives by two mottos: 'Keep a simple game simple' and 'Look after the small things and the big things will take care of themselves.'

'We don't want purists or theorists at Liverpool,' he told me with a dismissive wave of the hand. 'Football is a simple game but one of the hardest things in soccer is doing the simple things regularly.

'Take concentration. That's too easy to bother most so-called deep thinkers, but is it? Geoff Boycott stayed so long at the very top because of it. They decry him and say he's too professional but if Geoff Boycott were a foot-baller he'd be welcome here.'

Paisley's hidden ruthless streak made him the greatest exponent of the 'move 'em out' logic within the game. Paisley peddled many a big name at precisely the right time: Hughes, Callaghan, Heighway, Toshack, Lloyd, Ray Kennedy and Terry McDermott. It's another Liver-pool success secret — not letting sentiment and a stack of international caps get in the way of reality.

'The most uncomfortable job is telling kids they aren't going to make it,' said Paisley, 'but the hardest is selling established players. I can tell when they should go, but it's how they are going to take it.

'Emlyn Hughes thought he should be in Liverpool's first team because he was playing for England, but I knew he had knee trouble. It was time for him to move on. I unloaded Tosh at twenty-seven because he had injury problems and moved Larry Lloyd for the same reason. Cally had to go after playing 850 games for us. A model pro.

'A birth certificate doesn't tell me a player's age. The training ground and match day does that. That's how I knew when to unload. A player isn't necessarily finished when he leaves us — he's just finished here.'

Paisley used psychology in his handling of big Toshack when he and Keegan were scaring First Divi-sion defences to death.

'Tosh was carrying an injury and I knew he couldn't train as much as the others,' admitted Bob. 'But I couldn't be seen to play favourites so I used to tell him "Halfway through training I'll shout you over to take a phone call. Go into the dressing-room and take a breather." Many's the time Tosh trained only half a morning through those phone calls.'

When Paisley lost Keegan to Hamburg he came up with another winner, buying Kenny Dalglish from Celtic. Keegan and Dalglish are repeatedly compared, which is hardly surprising, but perhaps the most perceptive comparison of these two world class stars comes from the man on the inside, Paisley himself.

Certainly Paisley's words in his autobiography are the most graphic I've read and I repeat them here:

'They are players of contrasting styles. Kevin is a bustling, hustling player who employs his tremendous energy and physique to twist in all directions whereas Kenny's anticipation allows him to turn players in one smooth movement. Kevin likes to run with the ball and carry it, while Kenny is a purveyor of it. He likes to have people around him so that he can use his vision. Kevin injects a racy tempo with his mobility, Kenny likes to stroke the ball around. The judgement in Kenny's passing bears the hallmark of great golf shots. And he can read ground conditions the way cricketers can. He has the uncanny knack of knowing a ball will bounce, carry or skid on a particular surface.

'Both Kevin and Kenny are quick — Kevin is physically faster. Kenny's first five yards are in his head as John Toshack had the first two yards in his head when he partnered Kevin. Just as Kevin had Tosh so Kenny formed admirable partnerships, latterly with Ian Rush but first with David Johnson whose strong running and mobility not only produce goals but also allow him to act as a decoy to move players around and create chances for others.

'Neither Kevin nor Kenny are outstanding at heading the ball but they are more than competent in the air and while Kenny reads what colleagues and opponents do, Kevin reacts to them — two differing techniques.'

Bob Paisley surrounded by all Liverpool's trophies.
Behind him hangs a painting of Bill Shankly.

Paisley concludes: 'I know one thing — I wish I could have had both of them as a manager. It would simply be a question of choosing the other nine players and a substitute and I'd expect to win the Grand National as well as cups and championships.'

Apart from someone who lives with a player day in and day out the best judge of a striker must be a goalkeeper. And England's Peter Shilton has no doubts about Keegan. 'A tremendous little finisher,' he says. 'He makes it hard for goalkeepers to read his shots because he hits the ball so quickly. He doesn't need to wind himself up to get maximum power. Another outstanding feature of Kevin's game is the way he creates shooting chances for himself — he's great at turning people and playing little one-twos with people in and around the box. Remember the way he combined with Trevor Brooking to score that magnificent goal in England's 3—1 win over Scotland at Wembley in 1979?

Bob Paisley shows off the message on his Anfield
wall: 'It isn't easy to stay on top.'

'And another thing you've got to watch out for are his
runs on the blind side of defenders. When he's around
it's fatal to have defenders watching the ball rather than
where opponents are running to off it.

'I well remember his goal against me when Liverpool
beat Leicester 3—1 in an F.A. Cup semi-final replay at
Villa Park in 1974 — it was a Keegan classic. There was a
long ball through the middle and Keegan, while running
forward, let it drop over his shoulder and then hit it first
time on the volley. I'm hard pressed to think of any First
Division striker who in that situation would have hit the
ball as early as Keegan did.

'I wore an all-white strip in those days and after the
Liverpool game Jimmy Hill suggested on TV that it
made it easy for Kevin to see where I was positioned. In
fact when I later discussed this point with Kevin he said
that he didn't actually see me until after he'd struck the
shot. It was an instinctive goal.'

CHAPTER SIX

Hamburg

KEEGAN'S DEPARTURE FOR HAMBURG was interpreted in various ways by different people. Tommy Smith, for example, stated that Keegan went purely for money. Brian Clough, on the other hand, seemed to suggest that somehow it was disloyal to leave England.

Smithy, the Anfield Iron, whacked the words in as fiercely as one of his tackles.

'Kevin's always had his head screwed on right. If you're talking about players worth £1 million, Kevin's like the Mona Lisa — beyond price. I admire Kevin for making full use of what he had. He could so easily have been another George Best, who squandered and wasted his talents. Kevin was a much more stable lad but he annoyed several people when he left by not levelling with them. All that about broadening his experience in Europe was just so much smokescreen — he went for the money pure and simple. And if he'd come out and said it no one would have thought any less of him but he acted as though he was ashamed of it.'

Clough, who has a knack of rubbing people up the wrong way, got stuck into Keegan when they were on the ITV World Cup panel together shortly after Kevin's move to Hamburg.

'Well, young man,' he drawled, 'who have you bet your deutschmarks on for the World Cup?' He then started ribbing Keegan for leaving England and because his wife was having their baby in Germany. But on this day Cloughie met his match. 'That terrific suntan of yours, you didn't get that by being patriotic,' replied KK. 'That didn't come from Bournemouth, did it?'

Any accusation about being unpatriotic stung Keegan. When he signed his two-year contract with Hamburg he insisted on a clause being inserted whereby he was released for all England's World Cup and European Nations Cup matches.

Some people might think that Bob Paisley is nearer the truth than either Smith or Clough. Bob told me: 'Kevin has a wanderlust. He has to keep moving on to new pastures and new challenges. He always has and always will.'

Certainly future moves to Southampton and Newcastle United appear to bear that out but at the time of his transfer to Hamburg Keegan stated that he was going because he was in a rut and playing almost from memory. He knew the entire Liverpool routine at corners, free-kicks, etc and with so many good players

Opposite page: Kevin Keegan signs for Hamburg watched by Liverpool chairman John Smith (left) and Hamburg's Peter Krohn.

around him the games seemed almost too easy. There was no incentive to improve. He felt part of a machine rather than an individual and consequently felt he must make a fresh start.

The facts of his new start are these: on his debut Keegan starred and scored in Hamburg's 6—0 win over Barcelona in a friendly match. He scored again when Hamburg beat Liverpool 3—2 at home in another friendly and got his first Bundesliga goal in the 3—1 destruction of Kaiserslautern. But when Hamburg, the European Cupwinners' Cup holders, took on European Cup holders Liverpool in the second leg of the Super Cup at Anfield it was a nightmare return to his beloved Kop for Keegan. Hamburg Kopped it 6—0 with Terry McDermott scoring a hat-trick.

Those are the facts but rarely do facts tell the full story. In reality the whole time was a nightmare for Kevin and Jean. Life was impossible — he was shunned by his new team-mates who obviously thought that they were a good enough team without this Englander who had won a European trophy the previous season. He couldn't speak a word of German and, to cap it all, the club put Kevin and Jean, plus their two old English sheepdogs, on the twenty-fifth floor of the Hamburg Plaza Hotel instead of in a house with a large garden as stipulated in his contract. As though that wasn't enough Hamburg's business manager, Dr Peter Khron, who had signed Keegan, antagonised the rest of the players by saying things in the newspapers like: 'With God and Kevin Keegan we will win.'

Team talks were comical with coach Rudi Gutendorf conducting them in three languages — German, English for Keegan, and French for Yugoslavian Ivan Buljan.

After only four months both Khron and Gutendorf left

and the rumour was that Keegan could follow them if Hamburg could get their money back. It was more than even the resilient Keegan could take and everything finally exploded on New Year's Eve when Hamburg played a friendly at Lubeck, an ancient Hanseatic town about forty miles away.

Kevin recalls it well: 'A mate of mine from home had come over and was at the game. I'd left him a ticket on the gate but he couldn't speak German and couldn't make the bloke understand so he paid six marks, about £1.50, to stand with the Lubeck supporters. He'd just managed to push through to the front when — bang — I hit this left-back with such a left hook and right cross that I was off the field and he was scrambling to get out again. We both jumped in a taxi and shot off for Hamburg pretty quick.'

The man who took the full brunt of Keegan's frustrations was the Lubeck left-back Erhard Preuss.

In Kevin's first run Preuss punched him on the chin, smirking as he picked him up. Seconds later Keegan set off on a diagonal run off the ball and had his legs chopped from under him. He still hadn't touched the ball when the German got him again in the fourth minute sticking his shoulder into Keegan's chest leaving him doubled up and winded. The referee had taken little or no action so when Kevin dummied past Preuss on a through ball only to be hit for the umpteenth time something snapped inside. Keegan jumped up and struck him flush on the jaw knocking him unconscious.

'I thought I'd killed him,' he said later. 'I never bothered to wait for the red card. I sent myself off and walked straight into an automatic eight weeks' suspension from the West German F.A.'

Out of the dark often comes light and that was

97

certainly true for Keegan. Without him Hamburg lost seven matches, three of them at home and dropped from fifth place to the lower reaches of the table. A new realisation dawned on the Hamburg players . . . perhaps the new man had made a significant contribution after all.

Slowly but surely the dressing-room coolness was replaced by warmth and friendship. Team-mates began scanning advertisements for Kevin trying to find bargains. Results improved significantly, too, and the transformation was complete in 1978 when the West German players acutally voted him Man of the Year and he went on to win his first European Player of the Year award.

Keegan became the fifth British player to be officially voted Europe's best following Stanley Matthews (1956), and three Manchester United players: Denis Law (1964), Bobby Charlton (1966), and George Best (1968). He polled eighty-seven points followed by Hans Krankl (Barcelona and Austria) eighty-one, Rob Rensenbrink (Anderlecht and Holland) fifty, and Roberto Bettaga (Juventus and Italy) twenty-eight points.

One more year on — 1979 — and there was the ultimate in happy endings when Hamburg won the Bundesliga, their first championship for nineteen years. Kevin was top scorer with seventeen goals, an amazing haul for a midfielder, and literally ran away with his second successive European Player of the Year trophy. This time he polled 118 points, more than double his nearest rival.

It has always been something of a surprise to me that Kevin doesn't put those two European awards amongst his career highlights but he tells me that journalists merely voting for their top player doesn't rank with a European Cup winner's medal or captaining England.

Hamburg's Manfred Kaltz (left) gets away from
Nottingham Forest's John Robertson during the
1980 European Cup final in Madrid.

Maybe so, though I know of many an international footballer who would give his bank balance for one European Footballer of the Year award, never mind two.

Bill Shankly was certainly impressed at his protégé's
No. 1 ranking. 'Son, you've just climbed Everest,' he told
KK. Hamburg's response was more stark. 'Congratul-
ations,' they said. 'You've just been elected European
Footballer of the Year. Now here's your shovel, get out
and clear the terraces of snow.'

What Keegan does rate is the Hamburg team he
played in. After winning the Bundesliga they stormed
through the early rounds of the European Cup the
following season only to lose the final 1—0 to Nottingham Forest in Madrid.

'We should have won that game,' Kevin told me. 'If
I'm honest with myself I must rate that Hamburg side

higher than the Liverpool one I played in.'

Actually the final was a disappointing one with John Robertson striking the winner for Forest. Hamburg played into the hands of the big Forest central defenders Larry Lloyd and Kenny Burns and when they did prise open the defence Peter Shilton was immaculate. Three saves typified his excellence.

Save No. 1 was from Bernd Nogly whose 25-yard shot seemed to swerve slightly to Shilton's right around the penalty spot and then bent left towards the top left hand corner of the goal. Shilton, having had to change direction, went for the ball with his left hand but then, realising that he wasn't going to get there, brought his other arm across to give him extra momentum and pushed it away with his right for a corner.

Save No. 2 came from that flag kick. Horst Hrubesch flicked the ball on with his head and Milewski was poised to apply the finishing touch with a header from six yards when Shilton dived forward to punch the ball away. 'I was very proud of that save,' said Peter afterwards, 'firstly because I anticipated Hrubesch's header and secondly because of the speed with which I reacted to the situation.'

Save No. 3 saw Milewski even closer to beating Shilton when Keegan chested the ball down to him in the penalty area. He hit a perfect half volley which seemed certain to go just inside the keeper's left hand post. The ball kept low and Shilton saw it late but somehow got over to it.

Keegan became so fluent in German that he acted as Newcastle United's official interpreter, as well as being

Opposite page: Peter Shilton, who pulled off three crucial saves to subdue Hamburg in Madrid.

That controversial Forest partnership of Brian Clough and Peter Taylor.

captain and star player, when he went back to Hamburg in the summer of 1983, but he still smiles at those early faltering attempts to master a new language.

'Shopping was hilarious,' he says. 'I remember going into an electrical shop to buy a fuse but I didn't know the German word and tried to stumble through gesturing furiously. They brought me a plug. "Nein, nein," I said indicating something much smaller. The assistant disappeared and returned with a set of Christmas lights. By then I was so confused I just took them home and said to Jean, "Look what I've got you, darling. Nice, aren't they?" '

Hamburg's coach was Branko Zebec, a Yugoslav who played outside-left in the Rest of the World team which drew 4-4 with England at Wembley in 1953.

Memories of him are still vivid — and painful. 'On some days Zebec would place a ball on the centre spot, sit on it, and set us off running round the track. We'd sprint down one side, jog across behind the goal, and sprint down the other side. He'd sit for an hour and a half while we ran and ran and ran. He'd send us round the track fifty times, a whole 100 sprints. I've never trained so hard in my life.'

What amazed and annoyed Keegan during his time in Hamburg was the way the West Germans slagged our goalkeepers. We feel we've probably got the best in the world in Peter Shilton and Ray Clemence but the Germans look upon English keepers in the way some folk in England love to joke about the Scots.

Clem is the favourite target mainly because if he has made a mistake more often than not it's been against West Germany or one of their club sides. Ask a German player about Clemence and he'll point to Bonhof's free-kick which won the match for West Germany in Munich in 1978 and the first goal on the same night when Ray got his angles wrong and the ball flew under his hand. He'll probably also mention Bonhof's goal for Borussia Munchengladbach in the European Cup quarter-final at Dusseldorf the same year. It came in the dying minutes. Clem started to crouch but the ball, a dipper, scooped up and hit his shoulder to finish in the top of the net.

Keegan, fiercely protective about his old Liverpool team-mate, didn't rate the West German keepers in return. He felt that outside of Sepp Maier and a couple of others the standard was poor. They were no more than shot-stoppers punching everything. Shoot from twenty yards and they would punch the ball straight back to you.

When the news got about that Keegan was likely to leave Hamburg in the not too distant future on the next stage of his soccer adventure the clubs began queuing up. Barcelona, looking to fill the huge gap left by the departure of Johann Cruyff, approached Kevin directly after an England match at Wembley which infuriated Hamburg boss Gunther Netzer. Real Madrid also put in their calling card while Juventus from Italy and American clubs New York Cosmos and Fort Lauderdale Strikers started rustling their dollars. English clubs, quite naturally, were casting envious eyes at the little man, with Chelsea leading the way. Southampton and Brighton from the First Division also made inquiries.

Liverpool were out of the hunt. True, when they had transferred Keegan they had agreed a deal with Hamburg which gave them first option to buy him back but that contract was now well out of date.

Around the Christmas of 1979 — two and a half years after he had left England — it became obvious that Keegan was to leave West Germany as well at the end of

104

Playing for England in West Germany in 1978, Keegan watches Pearson score with Ruessmann (No. 4) well beaten.

the season. Kevin phoned a bitterly disappointed Netzer from England, where he was spending Christmas, to break the news.

More than a month before Kevin had talked privately with Chelsea when he flew over to do promotional work for a commercial company at Stamford Bridge.

He said at the time: 'Chelsea are the only club outside of the First Division that I would be interested in joining. I have a great respect for Geoff Hurst. I like his style.'

Kevin's salary at Hamburg was around £125,000 a year but Real Madrid and New York Cosmos were prepared to double that to get him. Barcelona, in turn, were offering £1,800,000 for his transfer. Silly money was flying everywhere but significantly Keegan said: 'It's not all about cash. I'm now financially secure for life.'

In the early days of January Keegan dutifully announced the pecking order for his signature — Juventus were his first choice, he said, then Barcelona and thirdly Chelsea. No mention was made of Southampton where he was to end up.

Juventus quickly dropped out, beaten by their own clubs. Italy's thirty-two First and Second Division club presidents voted overwhelmingly to keep their 18-year ban on foreign players and the door was firmly slammed on the ambitions of Juventus. Only A.C. Milan, Napoli and Udiness had supported them. We were now exactly one month away from the Press conference at The Dell when Southampton sensationally announced to an unsuspecting world that they had beaten everyone to sign England's captain.

Lawrie McMenemy, a master at signing big name players, told me the inside story of Keegan's signing especially for this book:

'What sparked the idea inside me really was reading about Geoff Hurst going for Kevin. I thought to myself, "Bloody hell, if they think they can land Keegan surely I can." The first contact we had was perfectly legitimate. I was having a house built — the one we're now living in — and there was a long wall leading to the stairs. The architect wanted to put a light fitting on it but said the actual light was difficult to get because it was made in Germany. I said: "Give me the address of the manufacturers — I've a mate out there who'll get me one." I knew Kevin from working on TV panels with him and I gave him a bell. It was a genuine inquiry to get a light fitting quicker than we could at home.

'But one thing led to another and that was the first of

many calls. It was now common knowledge that Keegan was leaving at the end of the season. Even Hamburg accepted it. I was ringing at a time when Kevin's wife Jean was a bit down and the baby wasn't well. I felt they were both wanting to get people round them that they knew. So I kept dropping in things like,"I see Barcelona are interested in you. You'll need a bodyguard out there, mind you. It's dangerous in the public eye — did you see that so-and-so was kidnapped the other day?" It was all true but it was to my advantage to point it out.

'I told Kev that Southampton couldn't make him a financial offer to match Barcelona or Real Madrid but what we could give him was a bit of happiness. Keegan was coming over for an England game at Wembley so I arranged to meet him on the Sunday night at a house the club has in London. I took our financial director along with me but basically everything was still very much hush-hush. The rest of my board hadn't a clue about what was going on. We were dropping off the director's daughter on the way and we got terribly lost. By the time we arrived Kevin was already there. "I'm sorry we're late," I said. "That's okay," replied Kevin. "I'm sorry I've forgotten your light!" He'd left it in the boot of the car when Jean had driven him to the airport.

'I can picture Kevin now, sitting on the floor with his shoes off having a shandy. We talked and I must have put our case over well because at the end of it he said, "Give me a bit of paper, I'll sign now." I knew all the other bits and bobs could be sorted out later. Having Keegan's agreement to join Southampton was all that mattered.

'I kept the thing quiet for a few days before I told the chairman. There was then an agonising fortnight when plans were being made for the Press conference. It was a

107

lovely way of doing things. Liverpool knew what was happening because they had the original option, Hamburg knew and we knew. But not a word leaked out publicly. When Kevin Keegan walked into that Press conference you could hear the gasps from the reporters. It was a massive scoop.

'After it was all over — the interviews, TV cameras and that — we went back to our house and Kevin said: "Here's a present from me and the wife so you'll remember today." It was my light and it's still hanging on the wall today.'

CHAPTER SEVEN

Saint Kevin

THE PRESS CONFERENCE WAS HELD AT The Dell on February 11, 1980. Kevin Keegan was there with his wife Jean and the baby; Gunter Netzer had flown over from Hamburg; and Lawrie had invited Kevin's agent Harry Swales.

Southampton may be a soccer backwater; a town in Hampshire where the quality of life is the most important thing and where the directors politely offer you a sandwich and a drink of tea out of the best china cups at half-time. But Lawrie has a personality to match his appearance and 'the Big Man' had pulled off a few quality signings in the past — Ted MacDougall, Alan Ball, Peter Osgood, Charlie George, Phil Boyer, Dave Watson, and Mike Channon had all agreed to play for him. So signing another wasn't so surprising in retrospect though McMenemy admits: 'This was the best — he was worth two of the others on the field.'

The last obstacle had been cleared out of the way when Lawrie got rid of French club St Etienne, who had threatened to upset the apple cart.

The gasps of surprise and admiration when Keegan entered the room were as awed as if Lawrie had unveiled a Rembrandt or a Picasso and for a few seconds McMenemy allowed the media to drink it all in. His moment of personal satisfaction had arrived.

Keegan explained the signing by saying: 'My greatest ambition is to help England win the World Cup and I think it is very important that I should be part of the domestic scene during the build up. I know Southampton will give me the challenge that I want at club level. Obviously they cannot match the sort of money that Juventus, Real Madrid or Barcelona could offer but I know I will get enjoyment from playing for Lawrie McMenemy and that's what matters. Believe me, I can see Southampton winning the First Division championship in the not too distant future.'

Lawrie described the deal as: 'the greatest day in Southampton's history. It is even bigger than when we won the F.A. Cup in 1976 because the arrival of Keegan represents progress.'

'Within minutes of him signing,' said McMenemy's personal secretary Valerie, 'the phone never stopped ringing and the telegrams started arriving. They ranged from congratulations from little old ladies who knew nothing about football to a young lad who wanted, above all things, one of Kevin's old combs. There were estate agents by the hundred. Goodness knows how much they thought Kevin earns or is worth but one of the places offered was set in acres of land with its own helicopter landing pad, boat moorings, and even a separate house for the servants. He could have had as many cars as he

Pin up boys - Southampton pair Lawrie
McMenemy and Kevin Keegan.

wanted and we even had kennels offering to look after his
dogs during their quarantine period.

'We had offers of a special cake for his arrival and one
man had even written a song for the players to sing to
Kevin when he first arrived — can you imagine that?'

Keegan's transfer was not to formally take effect until
July 1 but Lawrie kept a piece of paper in his desk which
he showed to any foreign journalists and agents
doubting that KK was already Southampton's property.
'They can forget all about him,' he said. 'They could
offer me £10m and they still wouldn't get him. He means
more to us than just money.'

Going into more detail about Keegan's impending
arrival McMenemy went on: 'Kevin will always be in
demand because his strength is that he always gives good
value and never lets anyone down. But a strength can

also become a weakness by being too generous with your time. Therefore it will be rationed. I have experienced this sort of thing to a lesser degree and one of the attractions down here is that you can get behind hedges and relax a little bit more.'

In Keegan's first season at The Dell — 1980—81 — Southampton finished sixth from top of the First Division and qualified for Europe but his appearances were strictly limited through injury. He played only twenty-seven League games which brought him a more than respectable goals tally of eleven and made him second top scorer sandwiched between young Steve Moran (eighteen) and Mike Channon (ten).

'Kevin suffered from a ligament strain and he found it hard to live with,' said McMenemy. 'He became very frustrated because he wasn't used to being injured but his impact was unquestioned. For instance Steve Moran, whom I had introduced to the First Division towards the end of the previous season, learned his trade playing between Keegan and Channon. He was a very lucky lad.'

The following season saw Keegan at his dynamic, lethal best. He scored on the opening day at Nottingham Forest, got his name on the score sheet in all of the first four League matches, and never stopped scoring. By the second last day of January when Southampton won 1—0 at Middlesbrough through a Keegan goal — who else? — the sprightly Saints were standing at the very pinnacle of the First Division within sight of that championship KK had seen so clearly at his Press conference.

By now, though, Moran had been sacrificed with a back injury and the No. 9 shirt was being juggled between Puckett, Hebberd and Cassells. Keegan, in reach of the biggest of all domestic prizes, appealed for the club to buy before it was too late. Financially Southampton just couldn't respond and slowly, predictably, annoyingly, they slipped down the table to finish seventh.

But for Keegan 1981—82 was a personal success. He collected a superb twenty-six League goals from forty-one games which won him the Golden Boot award as Division One's top marksman. He was five goals ahead of his nearest rival, Alan Brazil, with Liverpool's Ian Rush, who scored a basketful in cup ties, managing only seventeen in the League itself. Yet to my mind the most stunning Keegan goal of the lot never even counted. Perhaps you were lucky enough to see it on television. It came in the 3—2 win over Manchester United when the ball was driven waist high from the right wing towards the inside-left position. It was dropping behind Keegan but he took off and, parallel to the ground, struck the ball viciously right-footed. It flew high into the net, unstoppable and unchallenged. Yet the referee chalked off one of the best goals ever seen on any ground in Britain because Spike Armstrong was standing in an offside position. Goals like that fill grounds but Keegan was denied his rights even though Armstrong was not interfering with play.

On top of his Golden Boot award Kevin was voted the Professional Footballers' Association Footballer of the Year — the players' player of the year if you like. He also came within a few votes of lifting the Football Writers' Association version for the second time, something I felt he deserved.

Ask McMenemy about Keegan's super season and he'll bluntly tell you: 'If he'd stayed he would have been even more successful. On one hand Kevin said that the club didn't sign enough players, then when we went out

Chatting away — from left to right author John Gibson, Lawrie McMenemy, Olympic athlete Brendan Foster and Kevin Keegan.

in the close season and got Peter Shilton to put the icing on the cake he said we couldn't afford both their wages. But that wasn't his problem. It was ours.

'However, I have no regrets about signing Keegan. For two years he did us proud. His is a special talent and in our team it blossomed to the full because I insisted on playing him right up front where he's at his best. Like most great players he gets frustrated when he's not seeing enough of the ball and wants to drop back but I've always believed in attacking football; getting forward and peppering the penalty area with crosses and shots.

'When you have a discerning crowd like ours who have to be lured in then you must attack. Usually we finish up the highest scorers at home in the First Division.'

While they were together at the same club McMenemy and Keegan were exceptionally close, much closer than the normal manager-player relationship. And their wives, Anne and Jean, became firm friends. Often big Lawrie and his star skipper would do personal appearances together all over the country. I was involved in one when they both flew up to the North East by private plane for their good mate Brendan Foster, the former Olympic athlete who was in the throes of making Gateshead one of the top athletic centres in Britain. It was a Sunday and all four of us did a lunchtime talk-in at a local social club before going on to the gymnasium next to the International Stadium for a session with schoolkids. Both Lawrie and Kevin went down a bomb as usual — their ability to communicate with young and old alike is one of their strengths. It was impressive stuff, too, with their pilot standing by to whisk them off to Leeds and their next public engagement. Two stars without a doubt!

Passion and commitment on the Southampton bench led by assistant manager John Mortimore and McMenemy.

The split was about to come, however. Though Keegan had signed a new contract in November, 1981, the World Cup finals in the summer of 1982 were to tear the heart out of the little fella and leave him desperately in need of a lift. That lift, Keegan felt, couldn't come from his usual surroundings.

'I knew what that meant and the enormity of the problem I faced,' said McMenemy. 'People like Danny Blanchflower slagged me off for not holding Keegan to his contract, which still had twelve months to run, but that shows they don't know the man as I do. With any other player bar Kevin Keegan a manager could have said "you're seeing out your contract" and that would have been it. But Keegan is an exception. He had made enough money to retire — to pack up the game. He never used that threat in so many words but I'd got to

117

know Kevin so well that I was aware of how his mind was working. He would have walked out of football if we had been stupid.

'No one — and I repeat no one — wanted Kevin to leave Southampton. Money was never mentioned when Keegan first came to me and said he wanted a new club. He made it quite clear that he hadn't the impetus to start again with us, to grind along for another season. I blame the World Cup for that. It changed things for him.'

Revealing the background to the transfer from Southampton's point of view McMenemy told me: 'I released him to play a special game in New York and I hoped that some club like the Cosmos would do a deal with him while he was there. In that way he would have continued to play with us until, say, the January and frankly half a season would have been better than none. But it didn't happen.

'Manchester United were Keegan's first choice and I gave them permission to talk to him, but they couldn't agree personal terms. Next were Newcastle United. And that was a ridiculous situation — there I was giving advice to Arthur Cox and Stan Seymour about how to sign Kevin and I was desperate to keep him myself. But if I had to lose such an outstanding player then I'm glad it was to my folk back home because I knew how much they would appreciate him.

'At a club like ours Keegan was loved after two years but he hadn't the adulation that he would have got at Manchester United or did get at Newcastle. There was passion on a Saturday but the rest of the week we could wander down the street quietly and uninterrupted. While that might have been an attraction at the start it wasn't in the end. He needed to get his adrenalin going again.'

McMenemy went on: 'Football really is like a religion in the North East and the big name footballers are looked upon as if they were gods. I remember discussing all this with Gordon Lee soon after he became Newcastle's manager. As an outsider he couldn't understand why almost every person he met in Newcastle only wanted to talk about football and why the Newcastle supporters placed such a big emphasis on watching so-called stars. Gordon is a good manager but maybe his football philosophy was at odds with that of Newcastle and Newcastle fans.

'I could understand it. Born and raised in Gateshead, I supported Newcastle as a lad (in fact I had a spell on Newcastle's books as a schoolboy) and that was one of the most memorable periods of my life. My friends and I didn't have enough money to watch all of Newcastle's games at St James's Park but that didn't stop us going there in the hope of a turnstile operator taking pity on us and letting us in for nothing. On many occasions I had to wait until ten minutes from the end of the match — when the gates were opened to let the spectators out — to get in!

'The economic climate in the North East was bleak, to say the least, and in those days Newcastle teams, filled with outstanding individuals like my favourite Jackie Milburn, provided many thousands of people with a Saturday afternoon escape from the drudgery of their Monday to Friday lives. Newcastle have tried to put the emphasis on star quality ever since.

'At a time when England is again going through an economic crisis, with mass unemployment, it's a pity that there aren't more Kevin Keegans in the game. His charisma was really driven home to me when Southampton had a friendly match in Casablanca. I

119

decided not to include him because he wasn't a hundred per cent fit but had to change my mind when I learned that he'd attracted a crowd of something like 73,000.'

It's worth looking at what happened to Southampton in the wake of Keegan's departure. Certainly if people were agog when he arrived they were furious when he left.

'Keegan came suddenly and went suddenly,' said Lawrie. 'And our supporters found it hard to accept. They had bought their season tickets in anticipation of seeing Kevin again and then — wham — before a ball is kicked he was away. It caused a tidal wave of feeling down here but I jumped on it straight away. I said publicly that if any supporter thought I'd conned them over Keegan I would walk out. They'd known me long enough to know I was speaking the truth.

'I hadn't forseen Keegan going and the team was unprepared for it. I'd let Golac and Channon go on frees and sold Baker to help finance the Shilton signing. Without Keegan as well the team wasn't good enough for Ball at his age, and so he went too. We just had to stumble along. Then came the awful business in Sweden when two of the players were accused of rape by a local girl. Times were tough — by December we were bottom of the League but I rolled my sleeves up and got stuck in and around April time we were on the edge of making Europe.

'The reaction of the fans over season tickets bothered Keegan. He came down afterwards and said he never realised what would happen and offered to do anything to help but, of course, there wasn't anything he could do.'

In a way the departure of Keegan and other established players like Channon, Golac and Ball — plus the

Above: Fan-tastic . . . the big man and king Kev.

Previous pages: Keegan, in Southampton's colours,
chases Sunderland's Pop Robson.

Sweden affair — was the making of McMenemy all over again. He had to prove the cutting edge was still sharp and hadn't been blunted by the passing of time and he did it brilliantly.

'When Kevin Keegan was here I wasn't stagnating but I was doing other things as well as management,' admitted the Southampton boss. 'With great players all you do is drop oil on the works and you know they'll do the rest. You walk around for half an hour during training so the lads start running a yard faster, you do your little tactical bit on a Friday, and then you turn up on Saturday to see great players play. If you have a good staff, as I have, it's even easier. This happened to Bobby Robson at Ipswich which is why it was right for him to get out and take over England. And it happened to me but I had the Keegan aftermath and Sweden to get me back in the groove.

'I had to get out there on the training field and I enjoyed it. Everyone worked hard to stop the boat rocking. And when the Swedish business came along I didn't have to look over my shoulder for trouble from the boardroom because it's not like that at Southampton. For a while when all the flak hit the papers I had to protect the players, put an arm round their shoulders and cuddle them. It was a dreadful time for us all. During that particular season — 1982-83 — I had to make two public announcements. One over Keegan and the season tickets and one over Sweden. If the incidents abroad had been as bad as the accusations I would have resigned because I was in charge of those players. But

Opposite page: Steve Moran, who 'learned his trade' playing between Keegan and Channon.

they weren't. Both players were found not guilty of rape.'

Southampton are now back on course and McMenemy proudly says: 'Players like Wright, Agboola and Wallace have come out of the ashes of Keegan's departure. Southampton's old boss, Ted Bates, who is now on the board, has said that the last two years have been my best in management. It would take another manager to say that because it isn't really reflected in results, but I know what he means.'

CHAPTER EIGHT

Playing for England

Kevin Keegan spent ten glorious years as an England international. His sixty-three caps span the years from his England debut against Wales in 1972 to his final appearance as substitute against Spain in the 1982 World Cup finals.

It was Lawrie McMenemy who once declared that the perfect balance for a football team was 'seven road sweepers and four violinists'. If that's so then Keegan was unquestionably one of the violinists. He helped make England tick; he made goals and scored them, and, above all else, he was captain of his country.

As the years roll by Keegan will rightly take his place alongside the England greats: Matthews, Finney, Charlton, Moore, Mannion, Wright and the rest. He will be remembered for his immense contribution to England's national cause at a time when they were trying to re-establish themselves after the heady days of 1966.

Not that the 36,000 fans at the Wales v England World Cup qualifier in Cardiff on November 15, 1972 were aware that they were witnessing the start of a long and magnificent international career by the newcomer on the right wing. England won 1-0 with a goal from Colin Bell but manager Alf Ramsey described the game as 'neither exciting nor entertaining', Keegan himself played indifferently.

Looking back he recalls the sudden transition from rookie striker to England international. 'I learned of my first cap from a friend who heard a radio bulletin and phoned me. I could hardly believe it. Only fifteen months earlier I had been in the Fourth Division with Scunthorpe and suddenly I was in the England team alongside stars I had watched as a schoolboy.'

One of those stars was Alan Ball, Keegan's hero in the 1966 World Cup.

'I spent three weeks glued to the television admiring this little redhead running around for England when clubs were telling me, "You're too small, too puny to be a pro," says Keegan. 'He was everything that I believed I was — he had the same build, he ran a lot, he had loads of skill and plenty of vision. Probably I am a shade stronger than Ball but basically that was me on the screen.'

With that sort of hero-worship no wonder Ball, referring to the game in Cardiff, was to tell Keegan years later: 'You were scared stiff.' Kevin remembers feeling like an intruder in the camp. The unspoken attitude was: 'Here's a newcomer, a young kid who has had a lot of Press exposure. Let's see him prove it.'

Opposite page: Keegan's first England manager Sir Alf Ramsey . . .

Sir Alf had told Keegan 'play as you do for Liverpool' but that was easier said than done. Martin Chivers didn't play at all like John Toshack at Liverpool and Rodney Marsh was a law unto himself. Keegan tried to operate between them but to no avail. What's more, he missed a goal with only keeper Gary Sprake to beat. 'I froze. Sprake psyched me out of it,' said Keegan later.

However Ramsey showed the sort of character which was a hallmark of his period as England's manager. He merely told Kevin to forget what he read in the papers. 'I'm sticking by you,' he said.

So Keegan was in for the next game, in January of 1973, against Wales again in another World Cup qualifier. This was Kevin's Wembley debut but the whole side froze round the penalty box and England went off to a chorus of boos having had eighty per cent of the game yet only managed a 1-1 draw. 'Nothing went for me,' he said. 'I went off absolutely drained by tension and by the effort of working twice as hard as I did for Liverpool.'

Keegan's first goal in a white shirt lay just round the corner, however. It came in his third international in May, 1974 against . . . you've guessed it, Wales. The youngster must have thought they were the only side England ever played!

It was in the home internationals and the first game in which Joe Mercer was temporarily in charge. Keegan was back at Ninian Park and, after Stan Bowles had put England ahead, he got the second. A simple tap-in but the feeling of relief pouring over him was all consuming.

So many players have found that being a class First

Opposite page: Alan Ball — Keegan's boyhood hero during the 1966 World Cup.

Division player doesn't make you an England star automatically. The transition almost inevitably is difficult. Keegan was no exception.

'I played almost twenty matches for England before finding my feet,' he said. 'I never imagined it would take so long.

'But perhaps it was a good thing because before I got my first cap everything had happened so quickly for me. Had I been an immediate success with England it might well have gone to my head. As it is I believe my slow international start helped my character and my career. Mike Summerbee took me to one side after my second game and told me this sort of thing could happen. And Colin Bell was another who took a long time to settle into international football. Yet when I went into England's team he was the man, the No. 1 England footballer and great to play with. Roy McFarland and Colin Todd were good but Bell ran the show.'

A month after his first goal for England Keegan ran slap bang into one of the most controversial incidents in his colourful international career. He was arrested and beaten up by police and security guards at Belgrade Airport.

They had over-reacted when some of the England players — not including Keegan — had begun larking about.

After getting out of Yugoslavia Keegan told the full story as follows:

'I was one of the first through passport control on our arrival from Bulgaria. I was loaded down with parcels and sat down on a bench and watched one or two of the lads larking about. One of the lads got on the conveyor belt. This fellow came and pushed him off and the next thing I knew was that somebody grabbed me round the

132

Colin Bell — he ran the England team when
Keegan was first selected.

neck. I reacted in the normal way but I didn't say a word. Two or three more fellows then joined in and I was dragged away.

'Before I was taken into a little room I was hit on the nose. It was still bleeding when they dragged me into the room and made me kneel in a corner and I was hit eight or nine times including being kicked in the stomach twice. It didn't really hurt that much but I was a bit shocked, as you can imagine.

'It wasn't until the officials of the Yugoslavian Football Association came in that they realised I was an English footballer. When they did find out they made me wash my face to get the blood off so that I didn't look so bad as I had in the room.'

A journalist friend of mine, Bob Harris, was on the trip reporting on behalf of Thomson Regional Newspapers and his account of the incident tallies perfectly with Keegan's.

The drama began when Frank Worthington, scorer of the winning goal in Bulgaria, accidentally walked into a plate glass wall rather than through the door. He was ribbed by other players over his clumsiness as the party moved into the baggage area. With no one there to direct, everyone moved through the first exit and Keegan, who had slept throughout the flight, sat on a bench while other players clowned around.

An official got angry when another Liverpool player, Alec Lindsay, climbed onto the moving luggage conveyor belt. He went over and began pushing the players out. Worthington, Lindsay, Mike Channon,

Opposite page: Frank Worthington — he walked into a plate glass wall in Belgrade Airport.

134

Keith Weller and Emlyn Hughes all left but Keegan, still weary, took a little longer to gather his collection of bags and souvenirs. The official then pulled him to his feet and while Keegan was struggling to regain his balance gave him a violent push. Other officials joined in and Keegan's passport was snatched from his hand and his baggage, including a coffee set he had bought in Sofia, was thrown to the ground as he struggled in the grip of a large uniformed policeman who had him by the throat while two others held his arms.

Angry England players, who refused to move from the baggage area until Keegan was brought back, demanded an immediate return home and the cancellation of the game, the final leg of England's three-match tour of Eastern Europe. Joe Mercer calmed the situation when he said: 'We can all go home, no problem. But Kevin won't be able to come with us. He'll have to stay and answer any charges. The only way we'll get him out is by sticking together and answering them back on the field. It's their country off the field but they can't stop us on it.'

The players backed Mercer's words to the hilt earning a 2—2 draw in front of 90,000 people with little Keegan emerging from his nightmare to devastate the Yugoslavs.

Keegan set up the first England goal with a corner which Maric failed to hold and Mike Channon scored from close range. Then, after the Slavs had gone into a 2—1 lead, up popped Keegan with fifteen minutes left to get the equaliser and one of the most satisfying goals of his England career.

If Belgrade was controversial and none of Keegan's

Opposite page: Caretaker boss Joe Mercer with Keegan's old Liverpool team-mate Ray Kennedy.

making then what happened a year later, in May, 1975, was equally controversial but very much of Keegan's making.

By this time Don Revie had taken over as Mercer's successor and Keegan walked out on him putting his whole England career in jeopardy. His club manager at the time, Bob Paisley, says: 'The chat Kevin and I had helped to heal the breach with Don Revie. Kevin came to see me at Anfield and, although I don't condone what he did, I fully understood his motives.

'On the previous Saturday Kevin had gone ahead and played for England against Northern Ireland in Belfast despite a death threat which had been made in a letter. But when Don announced the England team for the following Wednesday's game with Wales at Wembley it didn't include Kevin and what really upset him was that Don didn't say a word to him about it. So, eventually, Kevin packed his bags and left the England squad's hotel.

'Kevin and I had a talk about the situation and, again, I saw my job was to pick him up and lift his spirits. Don Revie telephoned, we exchanged points of view, and the axe was buried.'

Keegan said at the time: 'I think I've been used. I have been England's best player in two successive away matches but when I get a chance to play at Wembley I am left out. I'm sick about the way it was done because I thought I deserved better.'

In turn Revie explained that he had deviated from his usual practice of telling players individually why they

Opposite page: Don Revie — Keegan walked out on him then was made England skipper.

were left out because they were all due to go to the pictures and he wanted them to know the team before he gave it to the Press. The side against Wales was to be experimental with Keegan certain to be recalled for the big match against Scotland.

It all seems in hindsight to be making a mountain out of a molehill but whatever was the case it didn't sour Keegan's relationship with Revie long term. He admits to liking a man who was eventually pilloried himself for walking out on England and, indeed, it was the Don who first handed Kevin the England captaincy.

It happened in March, 1976 against the team that had figured so prominently in his England highspots, Wales. It was the final confirmation that he had been forgiven for his Wembley walk-out and Keegan had the best possible start as England beat Wales 2—1 with goals coming from Ray Kennedy and Peter Taylor.

Kevin admits: 'The appointment surprised everyone, not least myself, for only ten months earlier I had walked out on Don Revie. But Revie, always a man for detail, felt this particular team required a northern captain. So he gave me the job and I retained this honour for eleven matches.

'Then Ron Greenwood removed it from me, giving as his reasons that I didn't earn my living in England any more and that I was a forward, a bad position for captains. "Don't take it personally," he said, "but I'm giving the job to Emlyn Hughes." Although I saw his reasons I couldn't pretend not to be disappointed.'

Keegan has now captained every team he has ever played for, beginning as a 19-year-old with Scunthorpe.

He played for England under four different managers — Sir Alf Ramsey, Joe Mercer, Don Revie and Ron Greenwood — and it's interesting to note how he saw them from the inside.

Of Alf Ramsey KK says: 'Probably no football manager in history has never once upset a player but if such a paragon exists then his name is Sir Alf Ramsey. Has anyone heard a player slag him? I haven't.'

Though Keegan admits that he never felt at ease with Ramsey he adds: 'He was a players' man and he had the authority of someone who has achieved it all. When he entered a room there was a hush, a feeling of respect. When he spoke everyone listened, and what he said was always commonsense.'

Mercer, another man well thought of, took over England too late. He was entering his sixties but Keegan says: 'Going on tour with Joe Mercer was like going on holiday. "Enjoy it", was his theme. "You're here because you can play, so go and play. And if you want a beer, then have a beer." No England team for years had played with such freedom from strain. In his seven games Joe Mercer did our football a lot of good.'

Revie is perhaps the most reviled of England's bosses because of the way he quit. 'Don Readies', a man with a passionate love of money, negotiated with the Arabs behind the Football Association's back and signed for the United Arab Emirates. But in fairness it must be remembered that it was the same Don Revie who built a magnificent club side at Leeds United — a side which competed with Liverpool for the top spot for a decade.

'I hated Revie as Leeds United's manager,' says Keegan candidly. 'I played for Liverpool and hated everything about our arch enemies. Yet when I met him there was no difficulty about liking him and, as I began to know him, I saw that if I ever became a manager I would be more like Revie than any of the other managers I have known.

'Too many people talk about his faults while neglecting his strengths. He was always glad to help a charity or a good cause and that's something no one ever tells you about him. People say he wanted the best for himself but I honestly believe his main concern was the best for the players.'

Revie's dossiers were legendary, of course. Before an international he would compile a dossier containing a minute analysis of opposition tactics, strengths and weaknesses and playing habits. Each England player was given a copy to read and digest. I remember Malcolm Macdonald telling me how useful they were to prop a door open. Keegan and Channon used them for scoring pads when they played cards. But other players read them and re-read them until they scared themselves to death. Used for a casual look at your immediate opponent they were all right. But used to brood over they were dangerous in the extreme. Keegan admits that as captain he wishes he had told Revie: 'Burn 'em!'

Greenwood, the last of Keegan's England managers, was seen in this way: 'He combined qualities from all his four predecessors. His instructions were crisp and commonsensical like Ramsey's. His approach to football and encouragement of players were reminiscent of Mercer. He tried to be as helpful as Revie and looked for similar skills; and I suppose his Lillieshall background was owed to Sir Walter Winterbottom, founding father of the F.A. coaching scheme.' Keegan also liked the feeling of freedom Greenwood generated. 'We were on trust under him. It was no longer bed at ten as in Don Revie's days.'

Opposite page: Malcolm Macdonald being congratulated by Terry Hibbitt. Super Mac used Don Revie's England dossiers to prop open the door.

Ron Greenwood — last of Keegan's four England managers.

Greenwood eventually quit after the 1982 World Cup finals in Spain which also marked the end of Keegan's illustrious international career. But it could have been earlier had not Kevin, Mick Mills and Ray Clemence intervened.

England, you might recall, had a bumpy ride to the finals. They lost to Switzerland and the door looked firmly shut but then they went to Hungary and won 3—1 and suddenly roses were blooming.

Well, it was on the way back from Hungary that Greenwood dropped his bombshell. The champagne was flowing and the spirits were high when Greenwood, without warning, rose to his feet and faced the players in the aisle in the front section where England's party was separated from the Press and other passengers. The manager said: 'When I get to Luton, Dick Wragg, the chairman of the selectors, is going to be there to meet me and will announce to the Press' — and he paused — 'that I'm resigning. I made up my mind whatever the result last night.' He sat down and all around him was silence. The party was over.

His assistant, Geoff Hurst, went round the players and confirmed that Greenwood had decided to go. 'He can't do it,' was the response to which Hurst replied: 'Well, it's up to you to do something about it.' Keegan, Mills and Clemence as the senior players were delegated to approach the manager on behalf of all the players begging him to stay and it was agreed that once the plane touched down at Luton the bags would be forgotten and everyone would approach Mr Wragg to say they didn't want Greenwood to resign. They carried it out, too, and Greenwood did change his mind. Perhaps the most amazing thing of all, however, was that the travelling Press never cottoned on to the drama which had

Above: The auld enemy are beaten — Peter Barnes (centre) crashes home a goal against Scotland at Wembley in 1979 with Keegan looking on.

Below: This time Keegan beats Scotland's goal-keeper George Wood.

England captain Kevin Keegan beats Danish goalkeeper Birger Jensen to score the only goal of the
match at Wembley in 1979.

unfolded almost beneath their noses. The story never
made the newspapers.

So Greenwood, Keegan, Mills and everyone else set
off for the warmth of Spain in the summer of '83. It
should have been the highlight of Keegan's career. He
had always dreamed of playing in the World Cup finals,
the greatest stage of football, and at last, after the dream
had appeared to have been destroyed beyond redemp-
tion, it had been achieved. And Keegan was captain of
his country.

But instead of untold joy Keegan experienced frustra-
tion, sadness, and eventually deep misery. England aqu-
itted themselves well enough but it was without Keegan,
who was crippled by back trouble and only appeared in
the very last match and then only as a substitute.

There were rumblings that Keegan and Greenwood had quarrelled and though both parties publicly denied it Kevin's England career was to end under a black cloud in a way he never deserved.

The first hint of Keegan's troubles came during the home internationals before the team flew out to Spain. Shortly before England played Wales in Cardiff he got stuck in the bath with a back injury and returned home. And though he played in subsequent matches the trouble was soon to flare again.

Trevor Francis, who was to replace him in England's team, takes up the story: 'Five days before the opening game against France in Bilbao Kevin Keegan hurt his back at the training ground. He carried on but by the end it was troubling him. I didn't think too much about it but twenty-four hours later he was obviously in real difficulty with it affecting his walking and movement. I suddenly realised that I had a chance of playing; that he was doubtful, and Kevin himself told one or two of the others that he was pessimistic.'

The doubt about Keegan captured the attention of the world's Press more than almost any other item of team news among the twenty-four squads in the countdown to the start. Countless camera crews flocked to the England camp. Twenty-four hours before the kick-off Keegan had to give up and Greenwood announced his team. Francis was in with Graham Rix replacing Trevor Brooking, who had a groin strain, and the goalkeeping job going to Peter Shilton rather than Ray Clemence.

Keegan said: 'The back feels worse today than it did yesterday though I'm still hoping for a quick recovery. I think I have a chance of playing against Czechoslovakia on Sunday. Trevor Brooking and I, who are rooming together, know that those who have replaced us are good

Keegan is rescued from autograph hunters by an Italian policeman at Turin Airport after flying in with England.

enough to give us a chance of taking part later in the tournament. Meanwhile we've decided to put a red cross on our bedroom door!'

England beat a good French team 3—1 having had the bonus of a goal from Bryan Robson after just twenty-seven seconds. Robson added a second and Paul Mariner the third.

The storm clouds were now beginning to form for Keegan. The day after the France match he broke down again and the Press rumblings began. Greenwood went to great lengths to deny reports of a rift between him and Keegan and even talked of hanging one reporter 'from the nearest tree'. England beat Czechoslovakia 2—0 and again Francis takes up the tale: 'Keegan's back was now so bad that he was confined to his room, and the manager asked one or two of us to pop in and have a chat as "he's feeling very low". He was having to have his food taken in. He had been to see a local orthopaedic specialist without success. When I went to see him he was clearly in a lot of pain.

'The talk of a rift with the manager was totally untrue and, irritatingly, led to photographers almost camping outside the hotel.

Below: Keegan beats Hungary's keeper Ferenc Meszaros during the World Cup qualifier England won 1-0 at Wembley in 1981.

Opposite page: It's mine — Welsh keeper Dai Davies snatches the ball in front of Keegan (No. 7).

'Two days before we played Kuwait Kevin went missing. It was a well kept secret for none of the players knew where he was. We thought that perhaps he was in a clinic in Bilbao but the night before the Kuwait match the manager told us he was in Hamburg.

'The next we saw of Kevin was the following day at the training ground. He told me to keep secret the fact that he had driven to Madrid, a seven hour journey, to avoid the Press and had flown from there to Hamburg to see a specialist he had consulted before. By the next day he said he felt good enough to play.'

The West German specialist had obviously done a marvellous job because from that day to this Keegan has never suffered back trouble. When Newcastle United signed him shortly after the World Cup finals he was given an intensive medical because of his well-publicised back problem but passed with flying colours and battled through a full season without missing a match for that reason.

Kuwait bowed the knee to a Francis goal and England had qualified for the second round. Though both Keegan and Brooking had recovered to bring the squad up to full strength for the first time Kevin hadn't trained sufficiently to stake a serious claim for the match with former World Cup holders West Germany in Madrid.

Kevin revealed the sadness he felt in an interview on the eve of the battle of the great foes.

'Realistically, I have no chance of playing against the Germans and if the lads go out and win — and I hope they do — then there is no chance of the team being

Opposite page: Keegan at England's World Cup final headquarters at Los Tamarises in 1982.

152

changed except through injury. Hopefully they will carry on winning and that could mean I won't play in the tournament. I have always believed in the old maxim that you don't change a winning team. I have profited from it in the past and now sadly I'm a victim of it. I am surprised how I've been able to accept the disappointment. I try to look as if I'm happy. I almost feel like an actor, the way I have to hide my feelings.'

Germany smothered and contained and played out a 0—0 draw against England which meant, taking into account other results, that Greenwood's men had to beat Spain by two clear goals to reach the semis.

Speculation was rife that with Keegan at last fit he would come in for the crunch match, possibly for Francis, with his room-mate Brooking in for Rix. The situation became even more complicated when Steve Coppell developed knee trouble, the knee suddenly swelling when he was out playing golf.

Two days before playing Spain Greenwood gave the first hint of his selection when in a practice match he played Francis out on the right in place of Coppell and Keegan as Mariner's partner. That clearly looked like the plan if Steve was unfit, though Greenwood was keen to play an unchanged team.

The next day Coppell trained again but Greenwood delayed announcing the team telling the Press 'tomorrow'. That afternoon the England players were watching the Wimbledon tennis final which was followed by the Poland—Russia game and during it Coppell complained that he was in pain again, left at half-time, and went to bed. Greenwood then announced, totally unexpectedly, that there would be a team meeting at the end of the game on TV. When everyone gathered he said: 'Stevie's not well so Trevor

154

will be on the right and Tony Woodcock will be up front. Will Tony and Kevin Keegan stay behind please.'

'Over dinner the whole squad was agog,' remembers Francis. 'Between seven-thirty on Saturday night and the same time Sunday night Greenwood had changed his mind dramatically, leaving Keegan out. After training on Sunday morning he had admitted to the Press that it was the most difficult selection he had ever had to make. Could he have been influenced by Don Howe over dinner on Saturday night? It seemed the only explanation.'

The probable influence of Howe, I know, was certainly not lost on Keegan. After Bobby Robson was made England manager and Keegan was axed completely he was to mention Howe's name more than once.

England, needing goals, couldn't get them and at half-time Greenwood told his men: 'Keep going, if the goals don't come I'll probably have to make changes and try something different.' With eighteen minutes of the second half gone Greenwood threw on his old hands Keegan and Brooking for Rix and Woodcock. Five minutes later Brooking sent Robson to the line but his centre was flashed wide of the far post from five yards by Keegan.

England's most celebrated player held his head in his hands in anguish. Normally he would have buried such a header but the chance came too early; the game had already entered the desperation stage and Keegan was cold and unable to react positively.

The game ended 0—0, England were out, and a few of the players were in tears as they left the pitch. Not only Keegan but Brooking and Mick Mills, deputy captain in Keegan's absence, were never to play for their country

155

again. Leaving the ground England's coach was surrounded by a mob chanting 'Malvinas Argentina' and 'Gibraltar Espana' (it was at the time of the Falklands war) and although the police were in attendance a brick was thrown through one of the windows.

It was a sad goodbye to the world stage for Keegan. Everything had begun so positively and the scene had been set. Even though the numbering on the England shirts was in the main alphabetical the rule had been bent so that Kevin would wear his No. 7 in the same way that Pele always wore No. 10. He had been singled out as a special case; a star getting his just desserts.

But by the time the World Cup drew to its finale with Italy crowned the new kings, we were almost at Keegan's finale. All that remained was for new manager Bobby Robson to have his say.

Opposite page: Oh, the agony. Keegan after missing with a header during the 1982 World Cup finals when he went on as sub in the last match against Spain.

CHAPTER NINE

The Bobby Robson affair

When Keegan joined Newcastle United in the wake of the World Cup finals the fans were ecstatic because here, at last, was a star of genuine world status playing in a black and white shirt.

Not since Malcolm Macdonald bulldozed defences with all the subtlety of an air raid in the mid seventies had they had a current England international. Great local pride was felt when Super Mac scored all five goals for England at Wembley, even if it was only against Cyprus, shortly after he'd scored with a header against the much more impressive West Germany.

Before Macdonald you have to go back into the fifties to find Newcastle's last England star. That was Jackie Milburn, Wor Jackie to the faithful. A man still revered on Tyneside and still active in football as a journalist.

Now not only had United signed a player of immense stature but the England skipper as well. Praise be.

Any small, lingering doubts at the back of the mind that Keegan's injury-ruined World Cup could affect his international career were swept away for the supporters when new England manager Bobby Robson turned up on the opening day of the new season for Keegan's debut. In the past it's been a standing joke on Tyneside that England bosses only watch Newcastle play away because it's too far to travel to the North East for a game. But here was Robson, fresh as new paint, saying: 'This is an occasion in my homeland. I wouldn't miss it for the world.'

That quote from Robson — born in Langley Park — was like manna from heaven to United's followers and when Robson took his place in the directors' box he was given a standing ovation by the 36,000 crowd. The feeling was: 'here's a Geordie manager who knows his football. He'll look after Kevin.'

United won 1—0, of course, with a Keegan goal almost causing heart failure on the terraces and all seemed sweetness and light. Robson paid tribute to Keegan afterwards, saying he had lost none of his sharpness and his goal was a beauty.

What none of us knew at the time, of course, was that Robson had already made up his mind that England would have to live without Keegan. He was planning to rebuild for the next World Cup and older players like Keegan, Mills and Brooking were to get put on the shelf. Later, after the deed was done, Robson was to admit that his day at St James's almost changed his mind.

Opposite page: New England manager Bobby Robson is pictured taking his seat in the St James's Park directors' box to watch Kevin Keegan's debut for Newcastle United.

The crowd's reaction to Keegan and to himself, Keegan's response with a display of unbounding energy, and that goal, fashioned out of nothing, swayed England's new leader. But, once away from the passion of the North East, his head cleared and his thoughts returned to his rebuilding programme.

It was in mid-September of 1982 that Robson named his first England squad. Naturally it was eagerly awaited ... how would it differ from Greenwood's thinking? Would his Ipswich days be reflected in the party? Would there be any new caps?

England squads normally hit the sports desks of evening papers around 9.30 in the morning and, in anticipation of a back-page lead, I had arranged to ring Arthur Cox at Newcastle's Benwell training ground before 9.45 to tell him what was what. I asked if Keegan could be standing by to come to the phone afterwards for the usual quotes about being delighted to be in, etc. Arthur agreed.

When the twenty-two names for the European qualifier with Denmark a week later dropped on my desk there was no sign of Keegan anywhere. I phoned Cox immediately, passing on the bad news. There was a stunned silence while Arthur obviously got his thoughts together. Then the words came pouring out.

'I'm shocked — very surprised. This will annoy the whole of Tyneside, who have taken Kevin to their hearts. My immediate reaction to the news is "where is there someone better?" and the answer is that there isn't anyone. But this won't flatten Keegan — it'll act as a stimulant to him — he's that type of person.'

The official Robson reason for axing Keegan came over the wires: 'I've got to start somewhere as England manager. I have to map out a five-year programme. But

The men who acted — Bobby Robson (left)
and coach Don Howe.

I'm not saying this is the end for Kevin Keegan and Mick Mills — you can never write off players of true international class. I might well decide in the future that I need to turn back to more experienced players to steady the younger element.

'Leaving out Kevin was as difficult a decision as any manager has had to make. I had to make it after just twelve days in the job. It was almost as hard to leave out Mick and, from a personal point of view, more upsetting because I have known and worked with him at Ipswich for so long.'

After my phone call Cox pulled Keegan to one side for a quiet word. And then, realising that the Press would be following up what was a dynamic story, piled all the United players on a coach and left the training ground. By the time the TV cameras arrived with a posse of radio and Press men all that remained was Keegan's car abandoned in the car park. Kevin was to say next to nothing that day — apart from doing a column in *The Sun* newspaper. And that's what blew the lid off the jar!

In the column Keegan blasted Robson for not having the decency to phone him before making the decision public. 'Often in life it's the little things which let you down. Surely Bobby Robson could have phoned me. After being involved in the international set-up for ten years surely I'm worth a ten pence phone call.' Keegan went on to say he never wanted to play for England again. If Robson had almost closed the door Keegan shut it with a resounding bang.

In some quarters Keegan's stand brought sympathy, in others he was accused of being childish. I know, for example, that Bobby Charlton never received a call or thank you when his hundred-cap England career came to an end, but two wrongs don't make a right, of course.

What had stung Kevin was that the Football Association were more than ready to phone him in Hamburg and ask him to play in Northern Ireland when the ticket sales were going badly but they couldn't be bothered to do the same when it was time to say goodbye. He had an agreement with Hamburg to be released for all World Cup and European Nations games but not friendlies — hence the need for the F.A. to go on bended knee for his help in Belfast.

Mike Channon, Keegan's best friend in football, was at Newcastle on loan at the time Keegan got the elbow and he threw more light on the situation when he declared: 'I'm wondering if there is more to this than meets the eye. It makes me wonder just who is picking the team and what influence Don Howe has. Certainly I get the impression that Howe is no fan of Keegan.'

Those were significant words in view of what happened in Spain when Greenwood completely changed his mind over team selection for what turned out to be the last match against the host country. One minute Keegan was in, the next he was out and Trevor Francis, you will recall, felt the only possible answer was a conversation Greenwood had with Howe over dinner. Certainly in subsequent conversations I had with Kevin he showed little love for the England coach and felt he had a part in the final act.

While Robson set out to douse the flames Keegan remained unrepentant.

'I've no regrets about what I said. I felt I was justified,' he claimed. 'My record is there for everyone to see. On current form and goals scored I've done as well as anyone else who has been picked.'

Bobby Robson, local boy made good, was suddenly a traitor in the eyes of Newcastle supporters. His next visit to St James's was certainly different from the back slapping reception he got at Keegan's debut. The accidental meeting between the two principal actors in the St James's foyer was both curt and cold and afterwards, when the England manager left to go to his car, he was spat upon by some disgruntled fans.

Publicly he tried to do a Henry Kissinger stating that Keegan was 'one of only three superstars in my time as a manager' — the other two incidentally were George Best and Kevin Beattie — but all his endeavours were blown away in an eye-opening plea from Manchester United's Bryan Robson, the man Bobby Robson himself had picked to succeed Keegan as England's captain.

An injury-hit England squad was due to fly out to Budapest to take on the Hungarians in a crucial European championship match and Bryan Robson declared: 'I wouldn't hesitate in drafting in Kevin Keegan if I were Bobby Robson. His tenacity, courage, enduring skills not blunted by advancing years, and experience of international football would be a tremendous asset as we try to restore morale.

'I know that Kevin has said he will never play for an England team managed by Bobby Robson but he is big enough to bury the hatchet and seal any rift that exists. He could offer just the drive we need.

'I don't want to be accused of trying to pick the England team but I wouldn't be true to myself if I did not make an appeal for the restoration of Keegan. Kevin is only thirty-two, and a young thirty-two at that. He is a highly gifted performer and from what I have heard has lost nothing of his brilliance since moving into the Second Division.'

Such emotive words from a player of Bryan Robson's undoubted class were exactly what Bobby Robson could have done without. The England manager's brief retort was: 'I will do the job and select players. I won't listen to anyone else and that includes Bryan Robson. His remarks were rather untimely.' Privately England's new captain was told bluntly: 'Never do that again.'

CHAPTER TEN

Geordie pride

Newcastle united's chairman, stan Seymour, hailed Keegan's signing as: 'An occasion which will stand out in the club's history.' He added: 'Keegan has got something the public want to see. If the fans back us we will get right to the top. I'm glad we've got such a person. I'd like to think that my dad (Stan Seymour Snr) would have done the same. In my lifetime, and in the club's history, this is one of the occasions that will stand out as one of the greatest.'

Old Stan would most certainly have approved. He played alongside Hughie Gallacher in one of the best-ever United sides then, as chairman and honorary team manager, he pioneered Newcastle's great feat of winning the F.A. Cup three times in five years in the early fifties buying the likes of Frank Brennan, Joe Harvey, Bobby Mitchell and George Robledo. Young Stan had emulated his father in clinching the signing of a star of

What a way to start. Keegan scores against Queens Park Rangers on his debut for Newcastle United.

Keegan's stature and there is no higher praise than that. Bringing Keegan to Tyneside was like opening your own bank. The cash rolled in as supporters reacted to news which they found nothing less than sensational.

The day after Keegan's Gosforth Park Press conference the queues for season tickets at St James's snaked out of the ground. And Seymour celebrated by dropping his trousers — albeit not intentionally!

He was driving into St James's and past the crowds waiting to put their hard-earned money down. A few noticed him and pointed. Stan, happy to see United's supporters smiling again, jumped from his car to give them a wave and as he did so his belt caught in the steering wheel and he was left standing with his trousers round his ankles displaying his jockey shorts for all to see. Some wag shouted: 'I know you said you'd show your bum to the crowd if we signed Keegan but there's no need to, Stan!'

Joy was everywhere. Stan had his say, Keegan was bowled over by his reception, and even the normally sedate Arthur Cox allowed himself a smile as wide as the Tyne. As well he might.

Keegan had likened Cox to the great Bill Shankly, saying: 'He has the same grit and determination,' and Cox, in return, declared: 'I've got the best for the best,' referring to United's supporters.

The next step of course was for Keegan to play. And his debut couldn't have been a tougher match with Queens Park Rangers, most people's tip for promotion, at St James's Park. I was in the Press box with what

Opposite page: Mud, glorious mud. Keegan in black and white.

looked like half the world's football writers for the big occasion, and what an occasion it was.

There is no welcome like a Geordie welcome and this one was right from the heart. Several thousand people were locked out as the gates closed at more than 36,000 for a Second Division match and when Keegan led out United the noise was deafening. 'Kee-gan, Kee-gan, Kee-gan' reverberated round the ground as the little man who had won all the major honours waved happily to the crowd. He was hoisted aloft by two United supporters who had broken through the police cordon on the track and then the game was under way.

Rangers were destined to be the bit players in a drama of high quality but they tested a young and average Newcastle team which, before Keegan's arrival, had looked well short of promotion material. John Trewick, Newcastle's record buy at £250,000, was off injured inside a quarter of an hour and was never to play in the first team again that season. A goal took a long time coming but when it did in the second half it was enough to win the match and, as in all the best fairy stories, it was scored by the hero, Kevin Keegan.

In front of England's new manager, Bobby Robson, Keegan drove a low shot past Hucker at the Gallowgate end of the ground and ran on behind the goal to be smothered by team-mates and fans alike. 'I could feel the crowd sucking the ball into the net,' said Keegan afterwards.

It was a marvellous, emotional afternoon which, in some ways, camouflaged United's problems. No one

Opposite page: Newcastle centre-half Jeff Clarke, one of the successes in Keegan's first season.

could see past Keegan.

What was wrong was that Newcastle were short on class and experience and, over the next few weeks, the kids froze in front of big crowds rather than responding to them. The likes of Wes Saunders, Chris Waddle and Peter Haddock found it all too much and all were eventually dropped, as Newcastle frittered away valuable points.

What Keegan's signing did do, of course — apart from give them a damned good player — was give them status in the game. Other internationals wanted to jump on the Keegan bandwaggon and three more arrived in a relatively short space of time. Terry McDermott, who was in England's 1982 World Cup squad, came from Liverpool; ex-Manchester United midfielder David McCreery, very much part of Northern Ireland's valiant efforts in Spain, arrived from American soccer; and Kevin's big pal Mike Channon signed on loan.

I well remember being at Anfield to see Bob Paisley just before McDermott's transfer back to his old stamping ground and he was dying to sign on. Few people realise that Terry Mac dropped something like £300 a week on his wages just to get to Tyneside.

Keegan himself was inspirational. He played like he wanted to win the matches all on his own, covering every blade of grass and urging his team-mates on. The outcome was some good results, like the five-goal win at Rotherham when Keegan scored four with a breathtaking display of finishing. His first one was right out of the England top drawer — McDermott struck a marvellously weighted pass at inside-right which saw Keegan leave defenders trailing and whip the ball past a startled keeper. It was all good stuff, achieved, as it was, before millions on TV and against a team whose player-manager was Keegan's old Liverpool mate, Emlyn Hughes.

But Newcastle, chopping and changing their team, couldn't find the consistency needed to match their skipper. A back four that had begun as Craggs, Clarke, Haddock and Saunders became Anderson, Clarke, Carney and Wharton with only Jeff Clarke, a free transfer signing from Sunderland, being a consistently high performer. Channon scored on his home debut against Middlesbrough, turning away with that windmill rotation of the arm, but it was to be his only goal in a black and white shirt and he left at the end of the experiment stating that United were merely a midtable side which would never go up, even with KK. Later Howard Gayle, a Liverpool reserve, was hired on trial to play Channon's role but though he, too, scored he was not retained and later signed for Birmingham City.

To aggravate matters United tragically lost Keegan himself for five League games in the most bizarre manner. He agreed to play at Middlesbrough in a testimonial match for John Craggs and, turning quickly, completely out-thought Boro defender Darren Wood who accidentally poked him in the eye. The injury was diagnosed as a partially detached retina and Keegan was detained in hospital.

Keegan's last game before that injury was on November 13, 1982 when he scored both goals in a 2—2 draw at Leicester and his return was on December 27 when 30,559 turned up to welcome him back against Derby County.

The Geordies loved Keegan and treated him like a lord. They hadn't had a hero since Gordon Lee sold Malcolm Macdonald in the mid seventies and they kept faith with Keegan even though it was obvious that the

Malcolm Allison, who heckled Bobby Robson over
Keegan's England omission.

team wasn't in his class. United were playing in the Second Division against the likes of Shrewsbury, Cambridge, Carlisle and Charlton and, what's more, were never in a promotion position but still the crowds poured into St James's. It was, in its own way, one of the biggest compliments Keegan had ever been paid.

Twice the gates topped 30,000, for Keegan's debut and his comeback game. And four times 29,000 folk were present — for the games against Sheffield Wednesday, Carlisle, Chelsea and Fulham. Newcastle ended up with an average gate of 24,510, seven thousand higher than the previous season and way above the average of most of the First Division clubs. The bravery of Seymour and Cox in going for Keegan had been rewarded at the gate.

It seemed that every week the opposing manager and half of the players stated that Keegan was still good enough for England and called for his return. Certainly I had no reservations whatsoever — Keegan was still an exceptional star. The situation was so charged that I remember at a dinner given by the North East branch of the Football Writers' Association Malcolm Allison, who was sitting on the top table, actually heckling Bobby Robson during his speech. He wanted to know why Keegan was being ignored and was asking the England boss the question thousands would like to have put themselves.

The fans' respect wasn't confined to turning up at St James's. Letters flooded into the ground not just from the North East, or even the rest of the country, but from all over the world. All wanted Keegan's autograph and a little souvenir. United had to find a secretary to handle his mail but every one who wrote in received a personal reply from the star.

Newcastle got their act together somewhat after

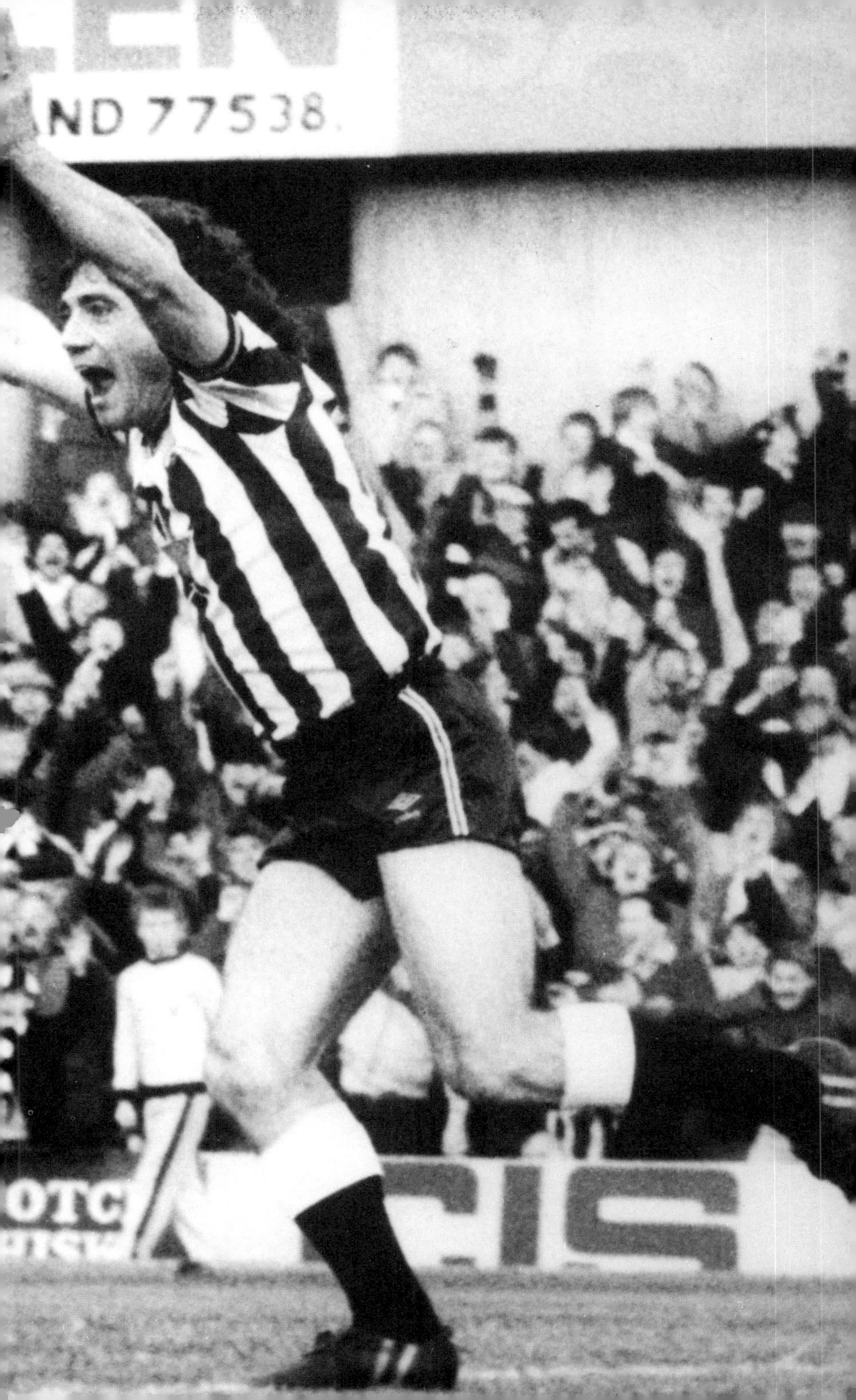
ND 77538.
OTC
CIS

Christmas and, from the beginning of April, they had a great run in. They lost only once in eight games to climb up the table and finish fifth behind the three promoted clubs — QPR, Wolves and Leicester — with Super Mac's Fulham fourth. Keegan finished with twenty-one League goals from thirty-seven appearances, a goal behind the overall total of his partner Imre Varadi. Not only his goals but his immense contribution on and off the park won him the North East Player of the Year award from the local F.W.A. and from my own newspaper, the *Evening Chronicle*. Typically, he thought it should have gone to his team-mate Jeff Clarke.

The whole of Keegan's career has been about success; about not settling for second best, and United's failure to win promotion at the first attempt needled him. He didn't want to be branded a failure at this late stage and he knew that if things stayed as they were Newcastle would probably fail again in 1983—84. Being a strong personality he tends to make his feelings known and this was to be no exception.

He had caused a few waves early on when some London Pressman had dared to suggest that Arthur Cox's job might be in the balance. Asked to comment Keegan simply said: 'If Arthur Cox goes so do I.' He had meant it to show a hundred per cent backing for a manager he respected greatly and nothing else, but one or two folk wondered if he was exceeding his power as a player.

The same question was asked following an exclusive article I did with Keegan towards the end of April. In it

Previous pages: How Newcastle United fans like to see Keegan — celebrating another goal.

Opposite page: Isn't life marvellous? Newcastle team-mates rush to congratulate Keegan.

183

he said that he wanted Newcastle United to sign class-players before he would commit himself to a new contract for the following season.

'I'm not holding a gun to their head but I want to see some movement from the club. I want to play with a better all-round squad next season so that we can gain more success. It's as much for the benefit of the fans as for myself. They deserve so much after all this time. The boss and the chairman know exactly how I feel so I'm not talking behind their back.

'I joined Newcastle because I have always put my faith in people not bricks and mortar, and neither Arthur Cox nor Stan Seymour have let me down. But at this stage of my career I don't want failure.'

To fully appreciate what he was trying to do you have to understand Keegan. His standards are exceptionally high and he expects other people's to be as high. He knew United weren't good enough and was trying to use his status in the game to help Cox get the men he needed to excite the supporters. He was giving the board and the bank a gentle nudge, if you like.

Immediately the season was over Newcastle embarked on a tour of the Far East, arranged because everyone out there wanted to see Keegan. It meant he had to play in all of the eight games in Kuala Lumpur, Bangkok and Japan.

In the land of the King and I — Thailand — Keegan was indeed a king. He was feted everywhere and was the

Previous pages: David McCreery, who joined Newcastle in the wake of Keegan's transfer.

Opposite page, above: Adulation . . . Keegan on tour in Bangkok.

Opposite page, below: Adulation . . . as he signs autographs at Don Muang Airport in Bangkok.

187

star attraction at a colonial style reception given by the British Ambassador. It was the same in Japan, where Newcastle were to play in the Japan Cup against the Syrian and Japanese national sides, Japan's crack club team Yamaha and Botofogo of Brazil. Though Keegan had never been to Japan his reputation preceded him. Full colour posters in shops, office buildings and on street corners featured him in the famous black and white strip to advertise the forthcoming Japan Cup matches. Tokyo newspapers, radio and television released daily bulletins on him and his Newcastle colleagues. Young girls stood outside United's hotel just to catch a glimpse of him, even the fact that he isn't tall was an advantage. Small is beautiful in Japan!

His importance was such that Keegan as well as the manager, Arthur Cox, had to attend all Press conferences after each game. The bulk of the questions inevitably fell Keegan's way.

Newcastle, as it happened, won the Japan Cup and were unbeaten on the whole tour. And such is the extravagant passion of their fans that more than 450 supporters lined the roof of the Newcastle Airport to welcome back the team. You'd have thought Newcastle had repeated their only European trophy success of 1969 when they lifted the Fairs Cup instead of merely winning a pot in a far-off land on a summer tour. Keegan wasn't even there, to the disappointment of the punters. He had dropped off at Heathrow to pick up his wife Jean and their two little girls, Laura Jane and Sarah Marie, before setting off for a family holiday in the sun.

The holiday was long overdue after what had been a busy few years for Kevin but, ironically, it was while he was soaking up the relaxed atmosphere of Spain that the biggest controversy arose. Keegan did occasional

Above: Swinger. Keegan on the golf course with
Terry McDermott (left) and manager Arthur Cox
(right). Note the Thai girl caddies.

Below: Sleepy time down south — Keegan takes a nap
on the shoulder of team-mate Terry McDermott.

columns for *The Sun* newspaper and it was decided to do another pre-season to help whet the appetite, so staff man Bob Cass flew out to see Kevin at his villa. The article when it appeared had all the impact of an H-bomb. It devastated Tyneside and temporarily split United's support right down the middle.

What caused all the furore was that Kevin voluntarily revealed the exact nature of the new one-year contract he was about to sign for Newcastle. In it were several escape clauses which would allow Keegan to leave United if promotion didn't appear to be on. If he bailed out at Christmas the transfer fee would be £75,000, between Christmas and the end of the season United would receive £50,000 and Keegan would get a free transfer at the end of the season.

Keegan tried to explain the unique contract by saying: 'The last thing I want to do is con the Geordie fans who made last year one of the happiest of my career. I'm signing the new contract on the understanding that the recent transfer movements will be followed by others. If we are going to achieve promotion while I'm here it will have to be next season.'

Kevin went on to say some nice things about the fans and the area and stated: 'You can put your house on us this time. This is going to be nine months to remember.' But the news that Keegan was staying was overshadowed by the details of the contract to be signed. Some United fans, who had already bought their season tickets on the strength of Keegan, felt betrayed. They felt he could dive off at any time if the going got rough and, having already

Opposite page: Do me a favour, ref. Kevin Keegan makes his point to the law.

moved his family back south to Hampshire after a year of living in the North East, the feeling was that he wasn't preparing for a long stay.

Others, blindly black and white and therefore blindly pro-Keegan, preferred to think that their hero was merely kicking the board up the backside. Keeping the pressure on for new signings to guarantee promotion by leaving the uneasy thought in the back of the directors' minds that if they didn't cough up, their prize asset could disappear in a puff of smoke.

Certainly Tyneside talked about nothing else. Keegan was page one news yet again — and in the summer too. It was such a delicate subject that when I rang the chairman, Stan Seymour, he asked to see me rather than talk over the phone. When I arrived at his sports shop in the centre of town he again refused to talk in front of customers — or at the football ground. So we drove round and round Newcastle in the privacy of Stan's car. His reaction was forthright. 'Keegan is a special case,' he told me. 'When he joined us originally he made it abundantly clear that it was only for one year. Now we have got him again — are we to be criticised for that? As far as I'm concerned I expect Keegan to be with us for the whole of next season.'

We talked privately of several other side-effects which might easily have a damaging effect. The over-riding question was why on earth had Keegan volunteered the details of his contract rather than merely stating he was to sign for another year and leaving it at that. The chance of a Press man stumbling upon such information was virtually nil. Yet in lots of ways it was typical of the man. Just as, in fairness, he had told Liverpool's fans that he was leaving at the end of the season he felt he had to tell United's supporters the truth as well. In neither case did he visualise the dramatic effect of his actions.

Keegan was hurt by the reaction to his article, there is no question about that. His relationship with several Press men deteriorated considerably because he felt that articles questioning his deeds were mischief making. He felt let down and misrepresented. And he was strongly backed by Arthur Cox, the man he in turn had backed the previous season. Cox said: 'Kevin Keegan's contract is unique because he is a unique person as he has proved many times. It can be said, I suppose, that he is applying pressure to directors and management but it has to be obvious that the most pressure — the biggest spotlight — will fall on Kevin Keegan himself. That pressure will not bother him because he absolutely thrives on it. He wants us to build something very special on Tyneside and he wants to be part of it. He is winding everyone up for a flat-out promotion charge.'

On his return to Tyneside a week later for pre-season training Keegan claimed that the clauses were actually inserted as a safeguard for the club. If promotion wasn't on and the gates slumped they could save his considerable wages and get some money back at the same time. The likelihood of Kevin walking out during the season was slim on two points anyway — his concern for his own image, which he is most sensitive about, and his sense of admiration for the Newcastle fans. He genuinely believes that the North East is the last untapped hotbed of soccer.

United, in the meantime, were getting on with the transfer business that Kevin and the fans demanded. Goalkeeper Martin Thomas, on loan at the end of the season, was signed permanently and two new full-backs were imported — Malcolm Brown from Huddersfield for £100,000 and England Under-21 left-back John Ryan from Oldham Athletic for £225,000. But it was the final piece of the jigsaw which set tongues wagging. In the very last week before the new 1983-84 season opened Newcastle sold their centre-forward and top goalscorer Imre Varadi to their big promotion rivals Sheffield Wednesday.

Varadi had scored forty-two goals in two seasons since his transfer from Everton — a splendid return — and was never as popular as he was the day he was sold. Newcastle fans love loyalty and the fact that he didn't want to go, plus his goals tally, made him the flavour of the week. The fact that First Division Watford nipped in to pinch the man United had lined up to replace Varadi — Cambridge's George Reilly — only aggravated the situation.

In reality, though both Varadi and Keegan had scored a lot of goals in harness they weren't really good for each other. Keegan liked the ball played to feet, using his first touch to beat people and play little one-twos. Varadi, with an awful first touch but blisteringly fast, liked the ball played over the top so that he could use his speed.

Nonetheless his sale was controversial, especially coming so close to the big kick-off. United missed out on Reilly and, in their bid to find a tall target man in the mould of John Toshack, took a long look at both Billy Hamilton (Burnley) and Trevor Christie (Notts County) before deciding not to buy. When money was put down for a forward it was neither for a tall player nor a target man but Peter Beardsley, a Newcastle lad who had excited a lot of good judges at Carlisle United before going out to Vancouver Whitecaps.

Beardsley, who has a touch like velvet, became an instant hit with the fans and, with Keegan bombing away as usual and Chris Waddle producing the most

194

consistent performances of his short career, United strung six consecutive League wins together. The secret was that all three front men could play; they interchanged repeatedly, and the ball didn't come bombing back to defenders or midfield men.

However, Keegan's considerable contribution could not be denied and it was recognised by his old boss Bob Paisley who saw the last of those victories, a 3—2 win over Fulham, when he was spying on the Londoners in readiness for Liverpool's Milk Cup tie.

Afterwards he said: 'If Newcastle win promotion forget about making Kevin Keegan Player of the Year — he'll deserve to be named Team of the Year. I know he keeps himself in perfect physical shape but the responsibilities he carries are too heavy for one person even if it is someone as special as Kevin. They should rename Newcastle Keegan United.

'He took throw-ins, free-kicks, doubled up as a striker and midfield player, scored one goal and created another. He had more touches of the ball than the rest put together. Kevin is playing as well as I've ever seen him even at an age when most players are looking for a less demanding stint.'

Quite a testimony to quite a player!

St Valentine's day 1984 dawned to banner headlines proclaiming: 'Keegan Quits Soccer'.

Both the BBC and ITV flashed the news round the whole of the country and every newspaper and radio station clamoured to serve up each little titbit of information. The shining Keegan career was almost over. He was to retire at the end of the season.

With the typical flair of a showman Keegan had chosen his thirty-third birthday — February 14 — to tell the world of his intention. The fact that it came slap bang in the middle of Newcastle United's nail-biting promotion push might have surprised a few folk not in the know, but in reality the timing was perfect.

Several clubs — most notably Portsmouth — had begun clamouring for Keegan's services, knowing that in three months' time he would be available on freedom of contract. Kevin was acutely aware of the devastating effect transfer talk would have on the hordes of United fans who travelled the length and breadth of England on the Keegan bandwagon. Desertion at the height of the battle was hardly the type of food to feed the troops. So he nipped the talk swiftly in the bud.

'I've made up my mind to retire and nothing will change it,' explained Keegan. 'I'm lucky to be able to quit while I believe I am still at the top. I want Newcastle's fans to realise that I won't be leaving them to play for another club.

'I'll kick the last competitive ball of my career in a Newcastle shirt. That's the highest possible tribute I can pay to a tremendous football public.'

His announcement didn't shock Seymour and Cox who had privately been alerted to it. But it produced a tidal wave of emotion in the dressing room.

'There's been no hint of this amongst the boys,' said Jeff Clarke. 'Everybody felt that Kevin wanted to go home to his family, but to stop playing altogether is a major surprise. He still has so much to offer.'

Clarke went on, 'It's terribly, terribly sad that at a time when football is crying out for personalities we are going to lose the Number 1. Even the Christmas annuals won't be the same after this.'

CHAPTER ELEVEN

What they said . . .

Famous people inspire or provoke strong reactions from everyone around them. It's natural, I suppose, and over the years Kevin Keegan has been the subject of many a profound statement.

If we look through KK's scrapbook there are some belters. Here are just a few to digest:

ARTHUR COX, Newcastle United's manager: 'Kevin is Roy of the Rovers. Some of the things he does no other player in the world can do.'

RON ATKINSON, Manchester United's manager: 'In the last decade the only world class players England have had are Kevin Keegan, Bryan Robson, the two goalkeepers Ray Clemence and Peter Shilton and, on their good days, Trevor Brooking and Trevor Francis.

'There's no doubt that Bobby Robson erred in getting rid of Keegan from the word go even though he was proving that he is his own man.'

A tense Arthur Cox (centre) with Newcastle
United's first team coach Iam McFaul (left) and
Peter Beardsley.

RAY CLEMENCE, England's goalkeeper: 'Kevin certainly had bare-faced cheek when playing for England. We were both on the bench back in 1973 when Poland held England to a draw and we failed to qualify for the World Cup finals in West Germany. With five minutes left Alf Ramsey turned and said, "Kevin, get changed." Keegan jumped to his feet and, in my excitement, I whipped his shorts and underpants down to his knees while trying to help him off with his tracksuit.

'That was bad enough but then it became clear that Sir Alf meant Kevin Hector and not Keegan. Hector got one of the briefest international run-outs ever — about ninety seconds — while Keegan was pulling up his shorts!'

MALCOLM MACDONALD, Fulham manager: 'It's only in recent seasons that Kevin Keegan has got what I would call a reasonable total of goals in a season. I found his scoring record at Liverpool disappointing considering the quality of the team.'

TERRY McDERMOTT, capped twenty-five times by England, commenting on Bobby Robson's failure to pick Keegan: 'It's criminal. Kevin should be on the plane before the pilot. He should fly it.

'Every team needs a Kevin Keegan. You could ask every player on that plane who they would like to be with them and every one would say Kevin Keegan. I've played with only two world class players in club football — Keegan and Kenny Dalglish.'

Following page: What a laugh — Terry McDermott grins up at Oldham Athletic goalkeeper Andy Goram.

199

Liverpool team-mate Joey Jones, in the international shirt of Wales, tackles England's Kevin Keegan.

JOEY JONES, former Liverpool and Wales left-back: 'I once got a rollicking from Bob Paisley for chopping down Kevin in an international "Don't forget you have to play with Keegan on Saturday," said the boss. I never forgot again.'

EMLYN HUGHES, Liverpool and England: 'When we roomed together we were always untidy. Once we deliberately overturned our hotel room because it looked so neat. We scattered clothes around everywhere and turned the furniture upside down. The hall porter approached us looking sick with worry when we returned from training. "Mr Hughes, Mr Keegan," he lamented. "Something terrible has happened. Your room's been ransacked. Would you check if any money is missing." '

Happy families — Kevin with daughter Laura Jane,
who holds dad's OBE, and wife Jean outside
Buckingham Palace in November, 1982.

THE QUEEN, when she bestowed the OBE on Keegan
at Buckingham Palace in November, 1982, commented
that he had been playing football for quite a long time.
'Yes, possibly too long, Ma'am,' replied Keegan who
insisted: 'This award is for my wife and family who have
been a great support for me and have had to put up with
my playing all these years.'

STAN SEYMOUR, Newcastle United's chairman, on the fact that Keegan earned £80,000 in his first year at the club: 'It's no secret that Kevin earns more than that figure in the balance sheet. There are promotional activities and he is on a percentage of the gate figures. But every penny is justifiable and I don't think there would be many people who would argue about that.

'On the gate share-out, let's face it, he is helping bring the extra fans in so we're making money not losing it. He is the major reason why our fortunes are changing. We were almost bankrupt a couple of years ago. No one can say anything about him not having earned his cash.'

ARTHUR COX: 'Keegan's an entertainer — just like Al Jolson was.'

TOM COWIE, chairman of First Division Sunderland: 'I wish we had supporters like Newcastle's. Their supporters are more loyal than ours. One has to be fair — if we had signed Kevin Keegan I don't believe we would have had the same reaction through the turnstiles.

'I would rather be in our position than Newcastle's but I would like to swap the fans.'

TREVOR FRANCIS: 'I was very surprised in an interview around 1979 when Kevin Keegan said he had never been able to get to know me, that I was very quiet and he wondered whether I would ever fulfil my potential. Certainly, I am fairly quiet but those who know me would say I am easy enough to get on with — at least, I would like to think that they would. He probably said what he did because he is the complete opposite to me. When we check in for a match I tend to say "hello" to everyone and go off to my room. Kevin walks in and bounces around full of confidence. We're all different and I was surprised he couldn't understand that.'

Fulham manager Malcolm Macdonald in full voice.

MALCOLM MACDONALD: 'I was selfish as a striker. I refused to hunt with anybody. I suppose Kevin Keegan summed it up best during the England-Cyprus match at Wembley when I got all the goals in a 5-0 win. When I knocked the third one in, Kevin came up to me and said quite seriously, "All right, you've got your hat-trick, how about making one for somebody else?" I said "Kevin, ———— off and get your own!" '

LAWRIE McMENEMY, Southampton's Geordie manager: 'I once thought I'd end up on top of Grey's Monument in Newcastle but now I suppose it'll be Kevin Keegan.'

TOMMY SMITH, Liverpool, talking about the England team in 1980: 'Ron Greenwood has to rely on certain key players to knit the side together and in that he's lucky to have world-class players like Keegan, Clemence and Shilton. Kevin Keegan stands out more than anybody for no one else seems to stamp the same authority on what they're doing on the pitch as he does. If anybody is needed to speak for England at the moment the Press usually go to Keegan or they talk about Clem and Shilton. Nobody sticks in my brain as being on the same par with them in this country.'

GORDON MILNE, manager of Leicester City, after Keegan had scored both Newcastle's goals in a 2—2 draw at Filbert Street: 'Keegan is still one of the best guys there is in the penalty box. He was an encouragement to everybody and his was a superb example in the art of finishing. He gave a great demonstration of how to pinch goals — he certainly pinched our pockets.'

JOHN TOSHACK: On the eve of the 1971 Cup final against Arsenal I telephoned my wife Sue at her hotel in London. She mentioned that the new lad who had signed the week before had carried her case for her from the train to the coach. She said that he seemed a very shy boy and that I should thank him when I saw him. His name was Kevin Keegan and I thanked him not just once but many times as the years went by.'

BRIAN CLOUGH, Nottingham Forest manager: 'I don't know whether it's right that Keegan is earning £3,000 a week at Newcastle but I'll tell you this — he deserves it. In fact, the way he's taking people's minds off problems like unemployment I think Maggie Thatcher's Government should chip in and pay him a bit extra.'

Happy birthday — Keegan gets a cake and a kiss from model girl Julie Parkinson watched by team-mate Terry McDermott.

APPENDIX

Cup Final Appearances

UEFA CUP

Final 1972—73

Liverpool 3, Borussia Monchengladbach 0
(at Liverpool May 10, 1973)

Liverpool: Clemence; Lawler, Lindsay; Smith, Lloyd, Hughes; Keegan, Cormack, Toshack, Heighway (Hall), Callaghan.

Borussia: Kleff; Danner, Michallik; Vogts, Bonhof, Kulik; Jensen, Wimmer, Rupp (Simonsen), Netzer, Heynckes.

Scorers: Liverpool — Keegan 2, Lloyd. *Attendance:* 41,169.

Borussia Monchengladbach 2, Liverpool 0
(at Monchengladbach May 23, 1973)

Borussia: Kleff; Vogts, Surau; Netzer, Bonhof, Danner; Wimmer, Kulik, Jensen, Rupp, Heynckes.

Liverpool: Clemence; Lawler, Lindsay; Smith, Lloyd, Hughes; Keegan, Cormack, Heighway (Boersma), Toshack, Callaghan.

Scorers: Borussia — Heynckes 2. *Attendance:* 35,000

Final 1975—76

Liverpool 3, Bruges 2
(at Liverpool April 28, 1976)

Liverpool: Clemence; Smith, Neal; Thompson, Kennedy, Hughes; Keegan, Fairclough, Heighway, Toshack (Case), Callaghan.

Bruges: Jensen; Bastyns, Krieger; Leekens, Volders, Cools; Van der Eycken, De Cubber, Van Gool, Lambert, Le Fevre.

Scorers: Liverpool — Kennedy, Case, Keegan. Bruges — Lambert, Cools. *Attendance:* 56,000.

Bruges 1, Liverpool 1
(at Bruges May 19, 1976)

Bruges: Jensen; Bastyns, Krieger, Leekens, Volders, Cools; Van der Eycken, Van Gool, Lambert (Sanders), De Cubber (Hinderyckx), Le Fevre.

Liverpool: Clemence; Smith, Neal; Thompson, Kennedy, Hughes; Keegan, Case, Heighway, Toshack (Fairclough), Callaghan.

Scorers: Bruges — Lambert. Liverpool — Keegan. *Attendance:* 32,000.

EUROPEAN CUP

Final 1976—77
Liverpool 3, Borussia Monchengladbach 1
(in Rome May 25, 1977)

Liverpool: Clemence; Neal, Jones; Smith, Kennedy, Hughes; Keegan, Case, Heighway, Callaghan, McDermott.

Borussia: Kneib; Vogts, Klinkhammer; Wittkamp, Bonhof, Wohlers (Hannes); Simonsen, Wimmer (Kulik), Stielike, Schaffer, Heynckes.

Scorers: Liverpool — McDermott, Smith, Neal (pen). Borussia — Simonsen. *Attendance:* 57,000

Final 1979—80
Nottingham Forest 1, Hamburg 0
(in Madrid May 28, 1980)

Nottingham Forest: Shilton; Anderson, Gray (Gunn); McGovern, Lloyd, Burns; O'Neill, Bowyer, Birtles, Mills (O'Hare), Robertson.

Hamburg: Kargus, Kaltz, Nogly; Jakobs, Buljan, Hieronymus (Hrubesch); Keegan, Memering, Milewski, Magath, Reimann.

Scorers: Nottingham Forest — Robertson. *Attendance:* 50,000.

F.A. CUP

Final 1973—74

Liverpool 3, Newcastle United 0
(at Wembley. Att: 100,000)

Liverpool: Clemence; Smith, Lindsay; Thompson, Cormack, Hughes; Keegan, Hall, Heighway, Toshack, Callaghan.

Newcastle United: McFaul; Clark, Kennedy; McDermott, Howard, Moncur; Smith (Gibb), Cassidy, Macdonald, Tudor, Hibbitt.

Scorers: Liverpool — Keegan 2, Heighway.

Championships, Awards and Caps

FIRST DIVISION championships with
Liverpool: 1972—73; 1975—76; 1976—77

BUNDESLIGA championship with
Hamburg: 1979

ENGLISH FOOTBALLER OF THE YEAR:
1976

WEST GERMAN MAN OF THE YEAR:
1978

EUROPEAN FOOTBALLER OF THE YEAR:
1978, 1979

ENGLISH PFA FOOTBALLER OF THE YEAR:
1982

ENGLAND CAPS

LIVERPOOL: 1972–73 v Wales (2); 1974 v Wales, Northern Ireland, Argentina, East Germany, Bulgaria, Yugoslavia; 1975 v Czechoslovakia, West Germany, Cyprus (2), Northern Ireland, Scotland; 1976 v Switzerland, Czechoslovakia, Portugal, Wales (2), Northern Ireland, Scotland, Brazil, Finland, Italy, Holland, Luxembourg.

HAMBURG: 1977 v Wales, Brazil, Argentina, Uruguay; 1978 v Switzerland, Italy, West Germany, Brazil, Hungary; 1979 v Denmark, Eire, Czechoslovakia, Northern Ireland, Wales, Scotland, Bulgaria, Sweden, Austria; 1980 v Denmark, Northern Ireland, Eire, Spain (2), Argentina, Belgium, Italy.

SOUTHAMPTON: 1981 v Spain, Sweden, Hungary; 1982 v Norway, Hungary, Northern Ireland, Scotland, Finland, Spain (sub).

(63 caps, 21 goals)

UNDER 23 CAPS

LIVERPOOL: 1972 v Scotland, East Germany (2), Poland, Russia.

(5 caps)

FOOTBALL LEAGUE STATISTICS

	APPEARANCES			GOALS		
	F. League (and Sub)	League Cup	F.A. Cup	League	League Cup	F.A. Cup
SCUNTHORPE UNITED	120(+4)	3	14	18	1	3
LIVERPOOL	230	23	28	68	6	14
SOUTHAMPTON	68	3	5	37	1	2
NEWCASTLE UNITED (to end of 1982–83 season)	37	2	2	21	0	0

Keegan's luxury home in Hampshire.

Wor Stars!

The Newcastle Breweries Ltd., whose beers include the world famous Newcastle Brown Ale, and Newcastle United AFC join forces to provide the City with a football team worthy of its fanatical fans.

We are particular where we put the famous Blue Star. Usually it is to be found only on beers that make it the symbol of good cheer to Geordies everywhere.

But we're especially proud to see "wor stars" on the strip of Newcastle United and one of sports greatest ambassadors — that star in his own right — Kevin Keegan.

We raise our glasses to the man who has done so much to lift the standards of the game and to the thousands of loyal supporters who have responded to his inspiration.